MONASTIC WISDOM SERIES: NUMBER SIXTY-FIVE

Saint Mary of Egypt

A Modern Verse Life and Interpretation

Bonnie B. Thurston

Foreword by Sr. Benedicta Ward, SLG

α

Cistercian Publications
www.cistercianpublications.org

LITURGICAL PRESS
Collegeville, Minnesota
www.litpress.org

A Cistercian Publications title published by Liturgical Press

Cistercian Publications
Editorial Offices
161 Grosvenor Street
Athens, Ohio 45701
www.cistercianpublications.org

© 2021 by Bonnie B. Thurston
Published by Liturgical Press, Collegeville, Minnesota. All rights reserved. No part of this book may be used or reproduced in any manner whatsoever, except brief quotations in reviews, without written permission of Liturgical Press, Saint John's Abbey, PO Box 7500, Collegeville, MN 56321-7500. Printed in the United States of America.

1   2   3   4   5   6   7   8   9

Library of Congress Cataloging-in-Publication Data

Names: Thurston, Bonnie Bowman, author.
Title: Saint Mary of Egypt : a modern verse life and interpretation / Bonnie Thurston.
Description: Collegeville, Minnesota : Cistercian Publications/ Liturgical Press, [2021] I Series: Monastic wisdom series ; number sixty-five I Includes bibliographical references.
Identifiers: LCCN 2021033566 (print) I LCCN 2021033567 (ebook) I ISBN 9780879071219 (pdf) I ISBN 9780879071219 (epub) I ISBN 9780879071165 (paperback)
Subjects: LCSH: Mary, of Egypt, Saint. I Christian women saints—Egypt—Biography.
Classification: LCC BR1720.M33 (ebook) I LCC BR1720.M33 T48 2021 (print) I DDC 270.092 [B] —dc23
LC record available at https://lccn.loc.gov/2021033566
LC ebook record available at https://lccn.loc.gov/2021033567

In gratitude for the life and work and friendship of
Sr. Benedicta Ward, SLG
"I was a stranger and you took me in . . ."

Contents

Acknowledgments and Thanks Giving

A research project over a long period of time on an esoteric subject by an author not resident in a university is impossible without the help of librarians. I have been in debt to them all my life. When the project began, then research librarian at Pittsburgh Theological Seminary, Anita Johnson, was unfailingly helpful, cheerful, and willing to accompany me to lunch buffets at an Indian restaurant. When I moved permanently back to West Virginia, my college classmate and then director of West Liberty University Library, Cheryl Ryan Harshman, and her associate Alan Ramsey, behaved as if it were not troublesome to order articles from obscure journals from places as far away as Australia, and they did so with alacrity. When reading at the Bodleian Library in Oxford, I found everyone on the staff, especially those in the Radcliffe Camera, to be unfailingly helpful. (May the Readers' Café in Weston Library always have the best and cheapest cup of coffee in central Oxford.) My thanks to these and all librarians.

When he learned of my interest in Saint Mary of Egypt, the Rev. Dr. John G. Panagiotou began to send me information: Sunday bulletins for Lent V with icons of her on their covers and meditations on the back, information from the internet, and his own reflections on Saint Mary the Egyptian. One of the great joys of teaching is when a student becomes a friend and colleague.

Michael Woodward, publisher and editor of Three Peaks Press in Abergavenny, Wales, and fellow Thomas Merton scholar, tracked down and sent me a recording of John Tavener's opera *Mary of Egypt*, which I managed *not* to listen to until *after* I finished the manuscript of this book. My gratitude to Michael is immense for this gift and for publishing my first two small collections of poetry.

For a number of years I was privileged on occasion to share life with the Cistercian/Trappistine community at Our Lady of the Angels Monastery in Crozet, Virginia, where Sister Kay Kettenhofen, OCSO, is a gifted iconographer (and drives the huge, terrifying mowing machine). She wrote a beautiful icon of Mary of Egypt for me that now presides over my sitting room. Sr. Kay answered several of my questions about the making of icons and Mary of Egypt. Both were invaluable, as is her friendship and that of her community.

Once again, I have occasion for gratitude to Hans Christoffersen and Liturgical Press, this time for taking on another "hybrid" book as well as for our long and fruitful relationship. Thanks to Michelle Verkuilen and Tara Durheim for promoting the book, and to Ann Blattner and Julie Surma for its lovely design and presentation. Finally, and especially, thanks to Professor Marsha Dutton, executive editor of Cistercian Publications, for her exacting editing of the manuscript and her patience with its computer-inept author.

Although she might deny it, Sr. Benedicta Ward, SLG, is the *prima mobile* behind this study. I first encountered her work in *The Desert Christian: The Sayings of the Desert Fathers* as a post-graduate student at Harvard Divinity School in 1983 and moved on to her books on early English Christianity and spirituality. Her *Harlots of the Desert* whetted my appetite for Mary of Egypt. For a number of years I was privileged to live for several weeks alongside the Sisters of the Love of God, her community in Oxford. The first time I arrived, I nearly fainted on the stairs in the house on Parker Street when I learned that hers was the other flat in the house. She was a gracious and generous neighbor, and many of the illuminated memories of my three recent residences there are of our drinking tea, eating biscuits (preferably chocolate), and discussing theology, literature, and life. Sr. Benedicta was unfailingly interested in my Mary of Egypt project, inquired about it, and heard the first of the poems. She gave love and will,

I am sure, receive the Kingdom. For all I have learned from her considerable scholarship and personal graciousness, I gratefully dedicate this book to her and hope that its deficiencies will not be an embarrassment.

Foreword

This new account of Mary of Egypt is not only a readable story, but it contains the inner truth about salvation for all. It has become fashionable to look into accounts of saints to assess their historical truth and often to reject the accounts for historical inaccuracy. This account of Mary of Egypt offers a far deeper way of understanding a holy life from the past. It has often been said that it is through true stories that the deepest reality can be known. Aleksandr Solzhenitsyn wrote in "One Word of Truth," his Nobel Prize essay, "Not everything assumes a name. Some things lead beyond words. . . . Through art we are sometimes visited—dimly, briefly—by revelations such as cannot be produced by rational thinking."[1]

Among all the works produced in writing, the most influential are the works of the imagination, when what they affirm is truth: in drama, prose, poetry, music, or art. It is the integrity of the inner world that matters. It is noteworthy that the ultimate book for Christians, all four gospels, show that what Jesus most used to convey his teaching was the story, the imaginary account, the parable.

In this remarkable presentation of the story of Mary of Egypt there are few participants: the disciplined monk, the cheerful harlot, Mary the mother of Jesus, the lion who buries Mary, and the desert itself. The story was told and retold and given new forms for many centuries. What facts lie within the story of Mary are not its main interest—details were changed to make the theme

1. Alexandr Solzhenitsyn, "Nobel Lecture," www.nobelprize.org/prizes/literature/1970/solzhenitsyn/lecture/.

clear. The facts could and did happen in many places and times. In the words of Gerard Manley Hopkins,

> . . . For Christ plays in ten thousand places,
> Lovely in limbs, and lovely in eyes not his
> To the father through the features of men's faces.[2]

Poetry presents the truth that creation and recreation are the work of God in all times, places, and people, through vivid images, with redemption always valid and available.

With this in mind, Dr. Thurston has reversed the order of the story and first placed the story about Mary in verse, though it was originally told in prose from the view of the good monk Zossima. Next she has placed the story of Zossima, a monk ambitious for holiness and trying to earn it by his actions—fasting, solitude, prayer. He changes his understanding of values when he meets Mary, who has nothing of the sort: only God in the desert. The poetry here comes first, as a story of extremes meeting: the free-living Mary, the over-disciplined monk, linked because both want to hear the voice of God. Mary lost her humanity by putting herself and her sins at the center, as Zossima lost his humanity by concentrating on his own virtues.

The saints often seem inaccessibly good, not near our own mixed-up lives. But this author presents two lives, each a total mess. The story is non-judgmental. It's just about grace working for a man/a woman, a monk/a harlot: all they have in common is that both want to hear the true word of God to them, as they have made themselves, one deafened by his own works, one making herself deaf by too much noise of self. Neither relates to many other humans. For Mary, her only human contact is with Mary the mother of Jesus, as her protector and guide. For Zossima, his only contact is other monks, after Mary's death. In opposite ways

---

2. Gerard Manley Hopkins, "As Kingfishers Catch Fire," *Poems and Prose* (New York: Alfred A. Knopf, 1995), 18.

Mary and Zossima are both needy human beings. Their meeting is of two sinners—with the mother of God and the all-embracing persona of the desert, the place of ultimate solitude and silence, where the word of God can be truly heard and received.

In this remarkable book, Dr. Thurston shows the way to understand the truth of the story of Mary and Zossima. She places first the story's truth in verse, then the explanation in prose. It is not that the historical context is unimportant. It is analyzed and presented with care, but what is central is the eternal truth of redemption and mercy for all. Its value is summed up in the defense of poetry that Keats sent to a friend: "I am certain of nothing but the holiness of the heart's affections and the truth of the imagination—What the imagination seizes as beauty must be truth—whether it existed before or not."[3]

In this book we have the beauty of truth for all indeed.

Benedicta Ward
2021

3. John Keats, [On the Imagination and "a Life of Sensations rather than of Thoughts": Letter to Benjamin Bailey, 22 November 1817], www.poetryfoundation .org/articles/69384/selections-from-keatss-letters.

Introduction

Almost everyone interested in Celtic Christian spirituality knows the medieval prayer (perhaps apocryphal?) about the lake of beer. The speaker wants to invite the people of heaven, folks from all the parishes around, and "the three Marys of great renown" to join in drinking beer through all eternity. One Mary is the blessed Virgin, Jesus' mother, another is Saint Mary Magdalene. But who was the third Mary? When the prayer was first prayed, the hearers would have assumed it to be Mary of Egypt, whose biography in the early church, Byzantium, and the medieval period in the West was well known and immensely popular, especially in monastic communities.

Unfortunately, Mary Magdalene and Mary of Egypt have become, in the words of Julie W. De Sherbinin, "two harlots fused into a single symbol."[1] I once encountered exactly this phenomenon in a lecture on women in the Bible in which an icon of Mary of Egypt was presented as the Magdalene. De Sherbinin explains that "the tendency to confuse the two sinful Marys prevails in Western hagiographical art,"[2] in part because Mary of Egypt is now little known or recognized in the West. Today, unless one is either an Orthodox Christian, for whom the fifth Sunday of Lent elevates Saint Mary of Egypt as the model of the repentant sinner, or someone with an interest in monastic history and spirituality,

---

1. Julie W. De Sherbinin, *Chekhov and Russian Religious Culture: The Poetics of the Marian Paradigm* (Evanston, IL: Northwestern University Press, 1997), 13–14; quoted in Onnaca Heron, "The Lioness in the Text: Mary of Egypt as Immasculated Female Saint," *Quidditas* 21 (2000): 39–40.

2. Heron, "Lioness," 40; De Sherbinin, *Chekhov,* 13–14.

one is unlikely to know "the third Mary." It is time for her to be resurrected.

I have written about desert people—early Christian widows, John the Baptist, Celtic Saints, Charles de Foucauld, Thomas Merton—marginal people, those brave enough to choose to live "outside the camp," at the psycho-spiritual fringes. Mary of Egypt is one of the desert dwellers. I encountered her some thirty years ago in studying monastic history and spirituality and subsequently developed a great interest in (and, to be honest, devotion to) her. For the last fifteen years I have done serious research into her life as it has been told in many hagiographical accounts, beginning in the sixth century with *The Spiritual Meadow* of John Moschos, continuing through Greek and Latin lives and dozens of medieval verse lives in many vernacular languages, at least six in the British Isles.

Additionally, a great many icons portray her from Greek, Russian, and modern Orthodox hands. When I began to track her down, I was stunned by the number of scholarly studies on the manuscripts of her biography in many languages,[3] as well as by the beauty and the variety of ways in which iconographers tell her story and present her to the onlooker. I have sought out icons of Mary of Egypt and commissioned one that was beautifully written by Sr. Kay Kettenhofen, OCSO, of Our Lady of the Angels Monastery in Virginia. I was delighted to read that in *De imaginibus* John of Damascus (d. ca. 750) cites the conversion of Mary of Egypt as an example of the efficacy of icons.[4]

In reading versions of Mary of Egypt's life,[5] I was, frankly, often struck by what a juicy and rollicking good tale it is. Hildegard

3. See the bibliography for more information.

4. Patrologia Graeca, ed. J.-P. Migne, 94:1415–18, quoted in Hugh Magennis, "Conversion on Old English Saints' Lives," in *Essays on Anglo-Saxon and Related Themes in Memory of Lynne Grundy,* ed. Jane Roberts and Janet Nelson, King's College London Medieval Series 17 (London: King's College London, Centre for Late Antique and Medieval Studies, 2000), 307.

5. An accessible one is found in Benedicta Ward, *Harlots of the Desert: A Study of Repentance in Early Monastic Sources,* CS 106 (Kalamazoo, MI: Cistercian Publications, 1987). Other collections are listed in the Bibliography.

L. C. Tristram calls it "one of the most colorful and . . . one of the most controversial of the mediaeval saints' lives because of its treatment of extremes."[6] Here is a woman who turned from God in childhood, enjoyed a wildly immoral life, came to repentance by a miracle of our Lady's intervention, then lived an ascetic and saintly life into old age, and, when she died, was buried by a monk and a lion. Hers is a familiar hagiographical pattern: sin, awakening, repentance, sanctity. The narratives about Mary of Egypt are also full of familiar literary conventions, echoes of the Desert Christians of the fourth century, and allusions to Scripture. The narratives communicate a timeless spiritual theology, entertaining as well as educating; it is no wonder that they were so popular and have endured for so long. Shining through all this is Mary herself. While my interest in her has not been exclusive or obsessive, in the last several years she has consumed a fair share of my energy as a scholar and poet.

Overall, Mary's story does not reflect contemporary, mainstream attitudes. The narratives about her don't reflect modern psychological or theological thought. With monasticism, which had preserved the story through the centuries, it went out of favor in the Western church at the time of the Reformation. Much later, after the Enlightenment, psychology equated mental health with feelings of self-worth and with self-actualization. So, for example, parenting came to consist of affirmation rather than correction. In this environment, a narrative with the reality of sin and the necessity for repentance at its heart is unlikely to be wildly popular or even marginally appealing. Similarly, in a world in which traditional sexual mores are in flux, some readers might smirk at the concept of sexual purity. But early and medieval Christianity valued both repentance and purity and loved the story of Mary of Egypt, who came to exemplify both repentance and wisdom, as she always has in the Eastern church. Hers is a story of the mercy of God: "Her

6. Hildegard L. C. Tristram, Introduction to *The Legend of Mary of Egypt in Medieval Insular Hagiography,* ed. Erich Poppe and Bianca Ross (Dublin: Four Courts Press, 1996), 10.

sins, which are many, are forgiven" (Luke 7:47, KJV). She is living proof that none are so fallen that God cannot lift them.

Mary's was a well-known and often-told story in ecclesiastical literature, and its continuing popularity is attested by dozens of medieval verse lives. Orthodox Christians continue to venerate her and include her in liturgical worship, reading her life at the morning service on the Thursday of the fifth week of Lent, in devotional materials, and in icons. She is well known in the monastic traditions of both Western and Eastern Christendom. In the last fifty years there have been two French novels devoted to Mary[7] and two operas, one by Ottorino Respighi, "Maria egiziaca" (with libretto by Claudio Guastalla), and one by the extraordinary English composer, John Tavener, subtitled "An Icon in Music and Dance," for which Mother Thekla, then abbess of an Orthodox monastery in Yorkshire, provided the libretto. It was premiered at the Aldeburgh Festival in June 1992.[8]

Even setting aside the current conceptual/intellectual environment, I greatly doubt that this generation will be drawn to Mary of Egypt by either another long verse life or an opera. Alas. But because her story has such power and has been transmitted primarily in poetic form, I have undertaken a poetic retelling of it by means of a series of lyric free-verse poems, each of which depicts a key moment in her life.[9] I have taken license with the original verse narratives (which vary from telling to telling) in several ways. I have not followed the structure or chronology of

---

7. Andrée Chedid, *Les Marches de Sable* (Paris: Flammarion, 1981); and Jacques Lacarrière, *Marie d'Egypte* (Paris: LATTES, 1983).

8. I am profoundly grateful to my friend, Michael Woodward, editor of Three Peaks Press in Wales, for sending me the Collins Classic recording of the opera, as well as for publishing my first two collections of poetry, thus in effect launching this book. I wrote all of the poems in this book before listening to or reading the opera's libretto.

9. To my knowledge, there is only one modern English lyric devoted to Mary of Egypt: "Maria Aegyptiaca," by John Heath-Stubbs in *The Swarming of the Bees* (London: Eyre & Spottiswoode, 1950), 15.

the original narratives, which open and close with Fr. Zossima,[10] and Mary telling her story within his; I have instead inserted Fr. Zossima *in medias res*. I write imaginatively in the voice not only of an omniscient narrator, but also in the voices of Saint Mary of Egypt, the Blessed Virgin Mary, Fr. Zossima, a lion, and a scribe. I rely on earlier verse lives for basic information, but I also invent material. Many of my poems contain quotations from an earlier verse life or from Scripture, which I quote from the King James (Authorized) translation for the aura of antiquity its language provides; for the same reason I also occasionally include Old English kennings (metaphorical compound words).

The heart of this book is a collection of poems, a work of imagination, not history. For those who might be interested in a more scholarly and historical treatment of Saint Mary, I append a lengthy analytical essay and select bibliography. I am well aware—having both read and been told—that Mary of Egypt may never have existed. As scholar Jane Stevenson has opined, "Mary of Egypt was invented in Palestine in the sixth century. The fiction of which she is the heroine is very closely linked with the needs and preoccupations of her milieu, but . . . the story has continued to resonate to subsequent generations. Its success is peculiar." She goes on to say, "This story of a woman who went to extremes seems to have an astonishing amount of life in it."[11]

I do not find Mary's enduring popularity "peculiar," precisely because of the "astonishing amount of life in it." The antiquity and multiplicity of the sources for her life have convinced me that Mary is not a fiction. But I'm not sure it ultimately matters. Thomas Hill suggests that every *vita* is based on a radically historical claim, but that it is also profoundly unhistorical. Such

10. I have encountered two spellings of the name, "Zosima" and "Zossima." The more standard English usage seems to be the latter, so I have used it except when quoting sources that employ the former spelling.

11. Jane Stevenson, "The Holy Sinner: The Life of Mary of Egypt," in Poppe and Ross, *Legend of Mary,* 19, 20.

narratives, he suggests, bring together the reality of the miraculous event and its symbolic meaning.[12] A narrative may be profoundly true without being factual, as any number of classic novels and much good poetry attests. I agree with Srs. Katherine and Thekla, who did a widely quoted English translation of the life of Mary of Egypt, that in some cases the actual facts are irrelevant: "It is the eternal value which is in question, and the eternal need not be proved."[13]

What made the story of Mary of Egypt appealing in earlier ages, what accounts for its survival and staying power, is the fact that it addresses perennially fascinating and important subjects: human identity and self-knowledge, sexual expression, vocation, sin, repentance, humility, devotion. It is also a classic depiction of the maternal wisdom and benevolence of the Blessed Virgin Mary. All of this speaks not only to modern monastics, whose forerunners first recorded and preserved the story, but also powerfully to the rest of us, or at least to some of us who are Christian. In addition to the moving account of Mary's conversion experience that I have included, when Zossima enters the story, my version begins to evince concerns that have come into focus more recently, in particular those concerning gender. I depict those by highlighting the complementarity of the main characters and the reversal of their traditional roles, the latter of which is evident in the early accounts.

Mary is a woman whose sins were largely of the flesh (the common trope of the repentant prostitute), but whose *conversio morum* and repentance came not through the mediation of the masculine, institutional church, but through direct encounter with the Virgin Mary, Mary of Egypt's moral and spiritual opposite and

12. Thomas D. Hill, "*Imago Dei:* Genre, Symbolism, and Anglo-Saxon Hagiography," in *Holy Men and Holy Women: Old English Prose Saints' Lives and Their Contexts*, ed. Paul E. Szarmach, SUNY Series in Medieval Studies (Albany, NY: State University of New York Press, 1996), 46, 47.

13. Sr. Katherine and Sr. Thekla, trans. and eds., *St. Andrew of Crete (The Great Canon) St. Mary of Egypt (The Life)*. (Filgrave, Buckinghamshire; Normanby, N. Yorkshire, UK; Greek Orthodox Monastery, 1974), 22.

on-going guide. Throughout her converted life, Mary of Egypt's faith and prayer are under the direct patronage of Our Lady, to whom she frequently appeals. They deepen not only through desert asceticism (another common trope), but outside the worship and structures of the institutional church until the arrival of the monk, Fr. Zossima, near the end of her life. He hears her confessional autobiography and brings her the Holy Eucharist.

But at their initial meeting Fr. Zossima is no saint. Zossima's sins are primarily those of the spirit, of pride or *hubris*, and his life has been one of apparent moral perfection within church structures as he sought more and more rigorous monasteries, sensing that there was something more than what he had experienced. In encountering Mary of Egypt, he recognizes his shortcomings. His *metanoia* comes through Mary, whom, importantly, he also comes to love. She receives the sacrament at his hands, as he receives his humanity at her feet. In that encounter, which reverses the gender roles in Luke 7:36-50, he weeps.

Recent scholarly literature about the relationship of these two figures, some of which I find quite wrong-headed, has had a gender-politics field day with the story. Perhaps remarkably in view of the antiquity of its origins, this is a narrative of complementarity. The male Zossima as representative of the institutional church (*amt* or office), and the female Mary, representative of "unregulated" or "unorthodox" spiritual life (*charism*), each, in different ways, find their fulfillment or completion in the other. In the end, each needs the other, and both become positive spiritual exemplars for people in every age. In my reading it is Mary's character and development that dominates the narrative, provides its (initially prurient) energy, and accounts for its enduring interest. Monastic readers may find Zossima's failings and dilemmas equally riveting. But that is for you to decide after you have read Mary's story, first in the prose summary that follows, and then in the poems themselves.

The Life of Mary of Egypt:
A Summary

Mary was from a good, Christian family living near the Nile in Egypt. She was baptized as a child, and in her early years was a noted beauty, but hardly a candidate for sainthood. At twelve she left home for Alexandria, where she lived an "evil life," though not supporting herself as a prostitute, as she took no money for her favors. She enjoyed what she did. After seventeen years of this life she joined a pilgrimage to Jerusalem, paying her way by "being kind to" (or actively seducing) those on the sea crossing. In Jerusalem she joined a crowd en route to the Church of the Holy Sepulcher or Church of the Resurrection to see a relic of the True Cross, but an unseen force or power prevented her from entering the church. Having been repulsed several times, she found herself gazing at, then praying to, an icon of the Blessed Virgin Mary near the entrance to the church. At that point she realized how far she was from the woman whose name she bore and immediately experienced deep repentance. Having prayed to the Virgin, she was at last able to enter the church and venerate the cross. Then she heard a voice saying, "If you cross the Jordan, you will find true peace." At once she went to the Church of John the Baptist at the Jordan River, entered the desert wilderness, and for forty-seven years lived there in solitude and penitence.

We would know nothing of her story had not the monk, Fr. Zossima, also come to the Jordan in search of a stricter monastery. His life too illustrates important lessons. If Mary's sins are of the flesh, his are of the spirit, the sins of over-estimating himself and of spiritual pride. Following the Lenten practice of his new monastery, Zossima goes out into the desert wilderness, where he encounters Mary and where, upon their first meeting, she, in obedience to him, recounts her life story. Zossima, who thought himself holy, had come face-to-face with genuine holiness and perfected humility. One year later, in obedience to her, he brought Mary Holy Communion. After the two encounters with Zossima (which included the miracles of her levitation and walking on water), Mary died in the desert. Upon Zossima's third visit, he found her incorrupt body, which a lion helped him bury. Having kept his word not to tell her story while she lived, Zossima was now free to tell it to his brothers, who were deeply moved and edified; in response, they established a feast day for Mary of Egypt and eventually recorded her life.

For thousands of Christians throughout history, Mary of Egypt has epitomized devotion to the Virgin Mary, penitence, prayer, and God's mercy. Her story and Zossima's were first preserved by Christian monastics, who told it to encourage their own perseverance in lives of purity and humility. But it is not an exclusively monastic tale. For anyone who has ever jumped to conclusions about and unjustly judged another, or known or trifled with the sins of Mary of Egypt (sins of the flesh) or of Fr. Zossima (sins of the spirit), and thus *any* sin, theirs is a story of consolation with an eternally happy ending. It speaks to all who "have sinned, and come short of the glory of God" (Rom 3:23, KJV). If God could forgive Mary, the story suggests, anybody can be forgiven.

In what follows, I tell Mary of Egypt's tale again, hoping both that you enjoy it and that you find in it a lively depiction of God's mercy, which bestows "peace which passeth all understanding" (Phil 4:7, KJV).

Feast of the Nativity of John the Baptist
June 24, 2020
The Anchorage, Wheeling, WV, USA

A Modern Verse Life
of Mary of Egypt

To the Reader

I will make the wilderness a pool of water, and the dry land springs of water.

Isaiah 41:18

Hers is a tale
that was often told
by those long past
and better than I.
I tell it again only
for love of her
who loved the flesh,
but loved Him more,
who leads the way
across the Jordan
to live in the desert,
to find it paradise.

Preface

Listen with your heart,
If you would have God's mercy.
. . .

These who would love God,
Will receive great benefit from it.
If you listen to this story
It will do you more good than any fable.

The Life of Saint Mary the Egyptian, anonymous 13ᵗʰ-century
Spanish poet[1]

1. *Saint Mary of Egypt: Three Medieval Lives in Verse*, trans. Ronald Pepin
and Hugh Feiss, CS 209 (Kalamazoo, MI: Cistercian Publications, 2005), 117.

Mary's Origins

An Egyptian from the Nile,
of noble stock by my good parents
who baptized their babe,
coddled, educated, loved her,
and strove to raise her well,
I was their beautiful child,
but willful, wanton, lewd,
and soon licentious.

I gifted my parents with grief,
threw their warnings to the winds.
In the Name of God, my mother
admonished me with tears,
pleaded I pursue a purer path,
promised me a good husband.
My father despaired of me,
cursed the hour of my birth.

Do not blame my debauchery
on those who did their best
for their delinquent daughter
of serpent-sharp tooth.
I disdained, abandoned their love.

At twelve years old I left them,
took my lusts to Alexandria,
never saw them again.

Mary in Alexandria

At first the great, glittering
city impressed a girl child
from the Nile country:
all those majestic buildings,
great markets full of men
who were all on about
a big, old library as full
of doddery old Greeks
as some quarters were
of dusty old Jews, or
others of randy Romans.
Those suited (and used)
me better than scholars.
Oh, there were Christians,
pompous, hypocritical,
more interested in argument
than in lonely immigrants,
and in their famed church
with some relic named Mark.
Who cares if I can't bed him?
One bedfellow burbled on
about the neo-somebody's.

17

The only body I wanted
was a live and lively one.
There were plenty of those.
I threw away my spindle,
any lingering respectability.
There are pleasanter means
for a girl to make her way
in a great, imperial city.
People are the same,
and men want exactly
the same thing I do.

Mary Explains Why

I did not do it for money.
For that I begged.
I did it for lust.
I opened my flower,
spread its petals
for any who sniffed
around my garden,
garden of delights,
for more than one,
garden of the fall.

At its center,
my insatiable center,
was luscious fruit,
carnal knowledge
of good and evil.
I offered the choice
to all comers,
laughed, then moaned
as they put their hungry
hands to the plow.

Mary Crosses the Sea

They that go down to the sea in ships . . .
These see the works of the Lord . . .
he bringeth them unto their desired haven.

Psalm 107:23a, 24a, 30b

Seventeen years. A long stay
in a city like Alexandria.
I saw a mixed multitude
(Egyptians, Libyans, others)
head for the port's small ships.
So I tagged along among
young men on pilgrimage
to famous Jerusalem
whither the tribes go up.[1]
I asked a weathered seaman
who could board his boat.
"Anyone who has the fare."
Oh, I had the fare all right.
I *was* the fair, and used it.

---

1. Psalm 122:4.

They took me along for sport,
sailed at night by the stars,
and I by Satan's sextant.
The wind was willing.
The wine was plentiful.
I sang, sinned, enjoyed,
and was enjoyed by many.
The unwilling, I seduced,
shamed even sailors.
But for good God's plan,
the sea itself might
have swallowed us up.
But a favorable wind
and the hand of God
brought this harlot
to the home of holiness
and thrones of judgment.[2]

2. Psalm 122:5.

Mary Is Refused Entry

We walked the rocky way
up to Jerusalem, which,
after Alexandria, seemed
only a dusty backwater,
but was full of men wanting
what I offered. Some, I pursued.
A festival was afoot, something
to do with an exalted cross,
which everybody knows
only criminals climb.
In morning darkness crowds
jostled toward some church.
So I followed. Why not?
Who sees life-giving wood?
On arrival, like the others,
I fought fiercely forward.
While peasants poured
through the yawning doors,
I was thrice close enough
to kiss them, but pushed back,
prevented by something unseen.

Fatigued by the stress of striving,
I withdrew to courtyard's corner.
Standing so close to holiness,
and lifetimes away from it,
I suddenly saw my sinfulness,
knew I prevented my entry.
From the sundered depths
of my smitten heart, I wept.
Bitter, bitter sorrow.
Glancing up from grief's grave
I found myself eye to eye
with the Mother of God.

Mary Beseeches Mary

Beloved ever virgin,
clean and free of sin,
you have right to reject me
for my loathsome lust.
To none other can I turn
but you who bore Him
Who pierced your heart,[1]
Who bled for sinners.
You own a woman's body,
used yours blessedly
as I mine basely.
I see myself as I am.
Forgive my foolishness.
Lady, let the doors be
opened to unworthy me.
Let me see His cross,
gaze on the glory,
adore only Him Who
deserves my worship.
Allow me a glimpse
of the gracious gallows.

1. Luke 2:35

I shall be forever
yours to command.
Whither thou biddest,
I shall go.[2]

2. See Ruth 1:16.

The Blessed Virgin Mary Speaks

. . . weeping may endure for a night,
  but joy cometh in the morning.

Psalm 30:5a

I heard other pilgrims call her
"that little whore from Alexandria."
But I knew her burning was
of an altogether different ilk.
"She weepeth sore in the night,
of her lovers, none comfort her."[1]
She was an ember longing for Light.

Thrice the spirit of my Son
barred her from His door.
But I spoke to Him who loves
me and repentant sinners.
So He turned her toward
His universal mother's arms,
clemens, pia, dulcis.

---

1. Lamentations 1:2.

26

In me her heart's eyes saw
the imprint of nails and cross,
torturous instruments of true love,
sorrow and comfort of all the burning
who pass through death's waters
and, like Mary of Egypt, rise up
shining with reflected glory.

Mary Meets Christ's Cross

There is a tree planted by God which we call Love,

You there, you I see in its branches.

Br. Jacopone de Todi (d. 1306)

Holy Mary, Mother of God,
prayed for penitent me.
I was given leave to enter,
impelled into the church
that thrice denied me,
gazed on the glory,
worshiped the wood
of perpetual regeneration.
Lignum habet spem.[1]
I adored you, O Christ,
and I blessed you,
because by your holy cross,
you redeemed the world.[2]

---

1. "Wood hath hope."
2. These four lines are taken from the traditional Good Friday Liturgy.

The tree of life
my soul hath seen.[3]
I, haughty Mary,
Egypt's loveliest whore,
in the holiest place
kissed the dust of the floor.

Then I returned rejoicing
to His Holy Mother
and begged her be
my advocate and guide,
promised her my purity,
promised her obedience
to every word she said,
then heard a faint voice
as if from a distant place:
"If you cross the Jordan,
you will find rest."
Straightaway I repaired
to the desert to be repaired.

3. Paraphrase of the first line of the anonymous American hymn "Jesus Christ the Apple Tree," first published in 1784 and known in the beautiful setting by composer Elizabeth Poston.

Mary Crosses the Jordan

*. . . the woman fled into the wilderness, where she hath a place
prepared of God . . . .*

Revelation 12:6

Leaving Her church,
I was summoned by
a mysterious man who
offered (not took) from me
three silver coins.
I bought three loaves
from the bread man
who pointed my way
outside the city walls
toward the Jordan
by the Jericho Road,
the wilderness passage.
Fleeing like the serpents
John the Baptist chastised,
longing for fruit of repentance,
by sunset I arrived
at the Forerunner's Church,

prayed as one on whom
the axe has already fallen.[1]
I could not bear human touch,
nor entrust myself to a priest,
who is a man, not a eunuch,
so went down to the river
to wash myself in its holy water,
then received the Holy Meal,
supped on eternity's bread.
I slept on the ground
like the innocent I was not.
In the morning a little boat
ferried me across the river.
I passed to the other side,
seeking Him Who found me,
praying to His Mother
to lead me in Her ways.
I have walked, and waited,
for forty-seven years.

1. Matthew 3:7, 10; Luke 3:7-8.

Zossima's Origins

None was a better monk than I.
None excelled me in virtue.
I was the most humble of all,
having lived our rule
blamelessly since childhood.
When my mother weaned me,
I was given to the monastery,
lived the life fifty-three years,
when I began to be tormented.
Were there greater perfections?
Desert fathers who surpassed me?
When a word came to me,
"Go from your country
and your father's house,
to a land I shall show thee,"[1]
I followed to a monastery
by the Jordan River
where the Porter led me
to the Abbot who inquired,
"What do you seek?"
"Spiritual progress," I replied.

1. Genesis 12:1.

"A gift God alone gives,"
he wisely rejoined,
"but if a great palm deigns
to live among small shrubs,
stay, take our yoke upon you,
learn from the humble of heart."[2]

2. Matthew 11:29.

Zossima at the Jordan Monastery

I stayed, but did not find
their yoke easy, burden light.[1]
Some monks did not sleep.
All ate only barley bread,
drank dank river water,
in the fullness of time
feasted on fruit and acorns.
There was no salt, wine, herbs,
no property or possessions.
None wore linen, but
grating goat's hair robes
tied with ropes of hemp.
They ate the Word of God,
and it was sweet to their taste.[2]
They all burned brightly,
in the desert's darkness,
knew Him Who is world's light,
bread of heaven, living water.
Among them was only kindness,
care, joy, mutual love.

1. Matthew 11:30.
2. Song of Songs 2:3.

When Lent came, two stayed
to keep prayer in the church.
After a meal and Mass,
the rest signed themselves,
thus commended to God,
scattered into the desert
to dwell with devils.
Forty days and forty nights,
they fasted in the wild[3]
none knowing the place
or progress of any other.
On the Sunday of the Palms
all returned rejoicing, safely
shriven, anxious to praise
Christ's mighty rising.
In my time, I kept
this rule and practice,
and by God's hand,
alone in desert's depths,
I was drawn to her.

3. From the hymn by George Hunt Smyttan, 1856.

The Lion Watches

Like as a lion that is greedy of his prey,

and as it were a young lion lurking in secret places.

Psalm 17:12

I watched them meet,
the pompous old priest,
the wizened old woman.
Her I cared for.
She chose our desert,
persevered here,
flourished in her way,
came to love ours.
Even the snakes
leave her alone.

Deserts are hot places
that get cold at night.
When it was frigid,
I wrapped around her
as if I were a mere
Egyptian house cat.

She'd troubles with
males of her species.
Their females do.
If he threatens her,
though not worth
the effort for a meal,
I shall kill him.
But for now,
I watch.

The First Encounter

*. . . the angel of the Lord found her by a fountain of water
in the wilderness . . .*

Genesis 16:7

I do not like the desert
that scorches by day,
freezes by night,
is full of the unsavory,
inedible, and poisonous.
I thought what I glimpsed
must be one of those,
some horrible apparition.
Blackened body, wizened hair,
like a startled wild beast
it ran to desert's depths.
Bidding anxious fear subside,[1]
this old monk, no runner,
followed, called to it,
"Stop. Pray for, bless me."
In a dry stream bed, it,
who was a she, stopped,

---

1. "Guide me, O Thou Great Jehovah," William Williams, 1745, trans. Peter
Williams.

called me by my name,
as she turned from me,
begged a cloak to cover
her body's nakedness and
a blessing for soul's succor.
I gave my old monastic robe,
and thus we knelt there
in mutual beatitude.
Then, standing, she asked
this trembling priest,
"Why have you come here?
What do you seek?
How goes the church?"
I told her of peace,
begged for her prayers.
She, turning East, lifted
hands heavenward, then
as she prayed, rose
from earth, stood on air.
Kyrie Eleison.
I fell in fear.
Signing herself, she said,
"I am not spirit, but human
as you are, battle as you do
the Evil One against us."
My weeping washed her feet,
for the Blessed Mother's sake,
I asked her to tell her tale.

Mary Confesses to Zossima

In Holy Mary's Name,

the priest asked I tell my tale,

tell it all, withholding nothing,

asked of food, clothes, temptation.

I fear the telling more than the tests,

fear speaking will fan embers

of long banked, fierce fires.

But confession is cure.

Before, I laid my body bare.

Now I bare my soul's life.

"I hungered for Egypt, fish, cucumbers,

melons, leeks, onions, and garlic,[1]

for wine, singing scurrilous songs,

touching where men touched me.

1. Numbers 11:5.

But She Who sent me to this desert
did not abandon me to die here.
I put my mind's eyes before Her icon,
wept, begged, beat my breast
until the shining, Her enfolding light,
dispelled the perils of my heart's night.
The touch of scouring sand,
of scorching sun taught me
we couple for more than pleasure,
for more even than progeny.
We eat for more than the body,
hunger for what it cannot give.
Our Lord was desert-tempted forty days,
was forty days among us in risen glory.
For seventeen years I sinned in Alexandria.
For seventeen years I was desert-shriven,
lived like a beast to become an angel,
am now restored to primal purity,
no longer, and yet remain, a woman.
Bless me, Father, for I have sinned.
Go back to your monastery,
but tell no man my story.
Return to me this time next year,
bringing Christ's Body and Blood,
the inexhaustible food for salvation."

Zossima's Response

Having told the story,
spoken her sinfulness,
she begged me
to pray for her
then disappeared into
the desert's depths.
I fell to my face,
kissed the hollows left
by her hoary, holy feet,
then, as monks do,
praised God in Psalm:
"Blessed is he whose
transgression is forgiven,
whose sin is covered."[1]
She, who was naked,
God covered.
I, who was covered,
God exposed.
Glory to thee, Oh Christ,
who showed me
perfection's measure

1. Psalm 32:1.

in the faultless penitent.
In her dark mirror,
I saw myself clearly.
Thus I returned
to my good brothers,
and was silent.
But it was a long year
and a year of longing—
for her.

Mary Remembers Her Tears

She weepeth sore in the night, and her tears are on her cheeks:
among her lovers she hath none to comfort her . . . .

Lamentations 1:2a

So I told him my tale.
Did the holy father hear
the turning point was tears?

Jesus wept for Lazarus
then emptied his tomb.
Mary Magdalene wept
outside an empty tomb
then heard her name.

Weeping watered
seeds of love scattered
at Christ's death's door,
sown under the care
of a different Mary.

Weeping marks more
than misery, baptizes sight,

signals recognition:
we are not, nor is the world,
as we thought.

Tears enlightened
my heart's eyes,[1]
showed me myself
as I was, gave hope
of a saint's inheritance.

As many have and will,
I returned by way
of the weeping cross.[2]

1. Ephesians 1:18.

2. Weeping crosses were those set up by roads for penitential devotion. "The tyme will come when coming home by weeping crosse, thou shalt confesse, that it is better to be at home in the cave of an Hermit than abroad in the court of an Emperor" (John Lyly, *Euphues and his England* [1580], in *The Wordsworth Dictionary of Phrase and Fable* [Ware, Hertfordshire: Wordsworth Editions, Ltd., 1996], 1146).

Zossima's Year of Vigil

I thought myself a perfect monk
until I met penitence perfected
in one who had forgotten self.
She had no form or comeliness,
no beauty that I should desire her.[1]
Yet she is lodged in my heart
as if some missing part
craved reunion and healing.
Day and night I desired
her face, manner, humility,
yet kept my promised peace.
Lent arrived; monks departed.
Felled by fever, I kept to my cell
until the brothers returned
for Christ's Last, Holy Supper.
Then I gathered figs, dates, lentils,
the sacred Bread and Wine
from the Lamb's high feast.
The day far spent, I left
for the Jordan, to watch
for her for whom I hungered,

1. Isaiah 53:2

praying, "God in whom I believe,
let me see what I desire."[2]
"Do not send me away without
seeing her whom you once
allowed me to behold."[3]
"Do not let me depart
empty handed, carrying
my own sins for judgment."[4]
Fearing her forgetful or faithless,
this old man waited in darkness
of bridegroom for beloved.

2. Anonymous Spanish poet in *Saint Mary of Egypt: Three Medieval Lives in Verse,* trans. Ronald Pepin and Hugh Feiss, CS 209 (Kalamazoo, MI: Cistercian Publications, 2005), 153.

3. Paraphrased from Benedicta Ward, *Harlots of the Desert: A Study of Repentance in Early Monastic Sources,* CS 106 (Kalamazoo, MI: Cistercian Publications, 1987), 53.

4. Alice-Mary Talbot, ed., *Holy Women of Byzantium: Ten Saints' Lives in English Translation* (Washington, DC: Dumbarton Oaks Research Library and Collection, 1996), 89.

The Second Encounter

Ode 9 The Irmos Troparia

*Thou with thy strange life, living outside matter
and surpassing nature, amazed all the ranks of Angels,
and gatherings of men; for Mary, walking as on feet
outside matter, thou crossed the Jordan.*[1]

In the moon's watery light,
not asleep, my heart awake,
listening for the beloved,[2]
I sat on dry earth waiting
by the Jordan's waxing waters.
Wraith-like, she appeared
on the opposite shore, made
the sign of Christ's Holy Cross,
arose like Him, like Him
walked across on the water
bringing wholeness, holiness,
whispered, "Bless me, Father.

1. Sr. Katherine and Sr. Thekla, trans. and eds., *St. Andrew of Crete (The Great Canon) St. Mary of Egypt (The Life)*. (Filgrave, Buckinghamshire; Normanby, N. Yorkshire, UK; Greek Orthodox Monastery, 1974), 128.

2. Song of Songs 5:2.

Recite for me the Holy Creed,
and the prayer of Our Lord."
Then, on my trembling lips,
she placed the kiss of peace
and lifted water-parting hands
to receive the Holy Sacrament,
wept, prayed the *Nunc Dimittis.*[3]
Of the provided provisions,
she took but three lentils,
having, like Elijah, food to eat
of which I knew not.[4]
"Go in Christ's peace.
Return to your brethren.
Remember me, a sinner.
In twelve moons,
if the good God wills,
revisit the dry stream bed
where first we met."
And so saying, again
she signed the waters,
crossed on unmoistened foot,
disappeared into the desert.

3. Luke 2:29-32. A prayer used at evening and night Offices.
4. John 4:32.

Mary's Last Prayers

*He that goeth forth and weepeth . . . shall doubtless come
again with rejoicing . . .*

Psalm 126:6

Holy Mary, Mother of God,
You always led me well
by ways I knew not,
pray for this sinner now
at the hour of her death.[1]

Lord, now lettest Thou
thy servant depart in peace
according to Thy word,
for mine eyes have seen
Thy salvation.[2]

As those at Pentecost
knew new languages
by the Spirit's power,

1. A reference to the *Hail Mary*.
2. Luke 2:29-30a. The *Nunc Dimittis* of evening liturgies.

I who am unlettered
know Your Word,
not as a dead book,
but as living, active.
Move my hand
to write in sand
a message for Zossima.

I crossed the Jordan
with Your Body and Blood
on my wretched lips,
and depart having eaten
a last time from Your table.

Have mercy on me a sinner
who with parched lips
lisped Your Name
thousands of times.
Now, may I depart in peace.
Bring sinful, blessed me
to see You face to face.
With You, Who were always
my heart's deepest desire,
now I lay me down to sleep.
"Her soul left her. The angels received her."[3]

3. Pepin and Feiss, *Saint Mary of Egypt,* 156.

The Third Encounter

Another slow year passed.
At the twelfth moon,
I left for the dry stream,
the desert trysting place,
but in my haste, lost
my way, began to pray:
"Shew me, Oh Lord,
that angel in the flesh
of whom the world
is not worthy."[1]

The sun rose.
Opening my eyes
I saw our stream bed
and her, dead.

Behold, and see if there be
any sorrow like unto my sorrow.[2]
I mourned for myself, prayed,
"through Your holy mysteries

---

1. Ward, *Harlots of the Desert*, 54.
2. Lamentations 1:12.

You refreshed Your servant,
have opened paradise to her,
welcomed her to eternal joys,
in Your kingdom of light."
Then I saw a message in the sand:
"Return me to the earth I am
who died Christ's passion night,
His Divine Supper and Name
on my unworthy lips."
Signed: Mary of Egypt.
Mary, the worthy namesake
of her Mother and mine.

Weeping, glorifying God,
I set about to do her bidding.
But the ground was hard.
I had no tool but an old stick,
struggled to dig, grew tired,
and, looking up,
Kyrie eleison,
saw the lion.

The Lion at the Burial

At first I thought her only cold,
curled around my old friend
as I secretly had done before,
then knew she had departed.
I kept watch until he returned.
The poor, old monk had never
done a lick of real man's work
in his whole, cosseted life,
tried to dig a hole with a stick,
might as well have used a spindle.

So, for her sake, I went to him,
for he loved her as I have,
went neck bowed, pride aside,
peacefully licked her feet.
He asked for Christ's sake
I do what was my intent.
With claws never bared to her,
I dug the grave for the corpse.
There wasn't much to cover.

With a free heart, I carried out
this servile deed,[1] while he
washed her body with his tears,
wrapped it in his ragged cloak.

And that was that.
What more could we do?
We parted, a humbled monk
to his meager monastery,
I the noble, lordly lion
to my deserted kingdom.
As he will, I will miss her,
pilgrim in this barren land.[2]
She was good company.

1. Paraphrase of Flodoard of Reims, in Pepin and Feiss, *Saint Mary of Egypt*,
70.

2. From "Guide me, O Thou Great Jehovah," William Williams, 1745, trans.
Peter Williams.

Zossima's Last Word

. . . hitherto have I declared thy wondrous works.
Now also when I am old and grayheaded, O God,
forsake me not . . .

Psalm 71:17b-18a

Having done all I could

for Mary now lionized,

I trudged the long, lonely

way back to the monastery,

to tell my brothers all

I had seen and heard

from the beginning:

Mary's life, levitation,

water walking, lion's help.

The brothers marveled.

Abbot John wept.

All were greatly edified.

Encouraged by her example,

they amended their lives,

instituted for her a feast day.

I, too, am a changed man,
a better, humbler monk.
I keep the rule with love,
but the years are long,
a corner of my heart empty.
Ut quid, Domine?[1]

1. Psalm 10:1a. Why stand far off, O Lord?

The Lion's Last Word

Judah is a lion's whelp . . . he crouched as a lion,
and as an old lion; who shall rouse him up?
The sceptre shall not depart from Judah . . . and unto him
shall the gathering of the people be.

Genesis 49:9-10

I am not "a lion that is

greedy of his prey,

a young lion lurking

in secret places,"[1]

and I have been fond

of the two-leggeds since

the one called Gerasimus

plucked that thorn

from my painful paw.

I patrol the Jordan to help

those who dare to cross it

and enter my domain.

1. Psalm 17:12.

But I am not a tame lion;[2]
will not be trifled with.

In other worlds and times
I am the great solar keeper,
who channels divine energy,
the power of *shakti.*
His disciples call Buddha
"the lion of the *Shakyas."*
I am symbol of Saint Mark
and mighty Alexandria.
I am "the Lion of Juda,
the Root of David
who hath prevailed,"[3]
shall prevail, watch,
wait for my time of return
as the triumphant Lamb.

2. "[Y]ou mustn't press him. He's wild, you know. Not like a *tame* lion" (Mr. Beaver in C. S. Lewis, *The Lion, the Witch, and the Wardrobe* [London: Puffin Books/Penguin, 1950/1969], 166).

3. Revelation 5:5.

A Scribe's Postscript

Ode 8 The Irmos Troparia

I will remember the works of the Lord:
surely I will remember thy wonders of old.
I will meditate also of all thy work, and talk of thy doings.
Thou art the God that doest wonders. . . .

Psalm 77:11, 12, 14a

Good brother Zossima lived
in holiness one hundred years,
then departed in peace to go
to God, our Lord, and Mary.
His tale was long passed
by word of mouth.
Now, to edify, I write
Mary's story as best I can
from what I have heard,
telling nothing but truth
as it was told to me.
May God grant mercy
to those who read what
is writ by the poor hand

of this unworthy scribe.
"The Mother of the Light, that never sets, having
    enlightened thee,
delivered thee from the darkness of passions:
thence having been admitted, to the grace of
    the Spirit,
lighten, O Mary, those who faithfully
    praise thee."[1]

1. Sr. Katherine and Sr. Thekla, trans. and eds., *St. Andrew of Crete (The Great Canon) St. Mary of Egypt (The Life)*. (Filgrave, Buckinghamshire; Normanby, N. Yorkshire, UK; Greek Orthodox Monastery, 1974), 126.

Epilogue

The old dream dreams.
The young see visions.
Beyond male and female
two old people met, both
riddled by imperfection.
Each, in their own way,
crossed the Jordan,
found desert's paradise:
asceticism and chastity,
humility and humanness.
She embraced the church's,
he the desert's, truth.
She accepted grace
at the hand of a man,
he at the woman's foot.
The lion looked on.
The lambs sleep safely.

Let every sinner know this,

Who may be guilty before God,

That there is no sin

So great or so horrible

That God will not pardon

Through penitence and confession.

To anyone who repents from the heart,

God gives pardon.[1]

1. Pepin and Feiss, *Saint Mary of Egypt,* 118.

Further Exploration of
Mary of Egypt and Her Story

This modern verse life of Mary of Egypt began with a brief introduction on traditions about her life and a sketch of her story's development. Although that introduction is ancillary to the poems, some readers may wish to know more about the background of Mary's life and the liturgical, literary, and iconographic depiction and development of her story. Though far from comprehensive (hers is a story too rich for containment), the following material fills in some of the gaps, and the bibliography points the way for those who are intrigued by the woman and her story.

As primary sources attest, Mary was hardly the only ascetic saint in early Christianity, but as Efthalia Walsh notes, "Mary appears to have been the most widely known in Byzantium." She was "enormously popular" in the Eastern and Western churches, and her story "was first understood strictly as a monastic document, written . . . to teach monastics true humility. The tale was told not to exalt Mary for her own sake, but to contrast Mary's humility with the monk Zosimas's pride in his saintliness."[1] It was "one of the most colorful and . . . one of the most controversial of the mediaeval saints' lives," writes Hildegard Tristram, "because of its treatment of extremes."[2]

---

1. Efthalia Makris Walsh, "The Ascetic Mother Mary of Egypt," *The Greek Orthodox Theological Review* 34 (1989): 60.

2. Hildegard L. C. Tristram, Introduction to *The Legend of Mary of Egypt in Medieval Insular Hagiography*, ed. Erich Poppe and Bianca Ross (Dublin: Four Courts Press, 1996), 10.

The extremes were not only those of Mary's life, but those of Zossima's as well. Both made radical departures from one set of behaviors and attitudes toward life and spirituality to another. And while the story does celebrate "a monastic spirituality that is rigorously ascetic and contemplative,"[3] its appeal (which is that of any well-told tale about characters with whom readers engage and whom they come to care about) is universal: the reality of second chances or, in theological terms, the hope of salvation for the sinner. It's a good story that reflects sound theology, or it would not have survived. And survive it certainly did, as Mary of Egypt's appearance and staying power are attested by the church's liturgical calendars, in its iconography, and in literary history.

Beyond the historical existence of the heroine, a problem related to writing a brief study of Mary of Egypt is chronological: the long history of transmission of the tale and the changes that occurred in it over time. Rather than assume the burden of reference to every document in each period, I have tried to indicate in a general way whether the source, theme, or detail in the narrative is "early" (generally the period of the New Testament and Greek fathers) or "medieval" (the Latin fathers and thereafter), fully understanding the potential overlap of these two designations and their coarseness.

For a woman with obscure Egyptian origins, Saint Mary's life story got around. Her feast was celebrated as early as the late seventh century as far away from Egypt as Northumbria. Her life is still read at the morning service on the Thursday of the fifth week of Lent in the Orthodox Church, and, as the only woman celebrated on a Sunday in Lent, she is commemorated on the fifth Sunday, the Sunday before Palm/Passion Sunday. In the Eastern church her feast day is April first and in the West on the second (or occasionally the ninth) of April.

In the introduction to *Holy Women of Byzantium*, Alice-Mary Talbot explains that in earlier eras of the church, "popular veneration preceded official church recognition of the sanctity of a holy

3. Tristram, Introduction, 13.

man or woman."[4] Talbot notes that a local cult developed first as pilgrims came to the saint's tomb. The anniversary of the saint's death became his or her feast day, and a *vita* (life) was written or an icon painted, and "eventually the saint might be recognized by the local church hierarchy." She goes on to say, "But canonization in the strict sense . . . did not occur in the West until the tenth century, and in Byzantium only in the thirteenth century."[5] This is almost certainly the route that Mary of Egypt's sainthood followed. It is her *vita* with which this essay is predominantly concerned (although mention will be made in passing of the iconographic record).

The Literary History of Mary's Life

Efthalia Makris Walsh notes that there are three early versions of the life of the woman we know as Mary of Egypt. She is variously depicted as a former nun and virgin in a monastery (a story attributed to John Moschos, d. ca. 619), or as a singer in the Church of the Resurrection in Jerusalem who, fearing she would tempt men, retired to a cave, where a wandering monk encountered her and subsequently told her story (Cyril of Scythopolis, a monk who lived in monasteries by the Jordan river, d. ca. 560), or as the sexual profligate become desert anchorite, contrasted with Zossima who preserves her story (Sophronios, Patriarch of Jerusalem, d. 638).[6]

The transmission of Mary's story from Zossima's telling of it to his monastic brothers, through Greek and Latin written versions, to the numerous vernacular manuscripts of the medieval period and into our own day, is complex and convoluted. Because this verse life is in English, I briefly trace the transmission history in

4. Alice-Mary Talbot, ed., *Holy Women of Byzantium: Ten Saints' Lives in English Translation* (Washington, DC: Dumbarton Oaks Research Library and Collection, 1996), vii.

5. Talbot, *Holy Women,* vii.

6. Walsh, "Ascetic Mother," 61–63.

English, though it would be possible to trace her life in many European languages. A hundred known manuscripts of early Greek texts exist, as well as versions in Armenian, Ethiopic, Slavonic, and Syriac; at least five continental French versions, a number in Spanish, and five Norse manuscripts were recorded between 1250 and 1445.

Although Andrew P. Scheil thinks that the "text's appeal remains enigmatic to a modern audience," he suggests it was "apparently a compelling narrative for readers in medieval England, existing in Latin, Old English, Middle English, Old Norse, Anglo-Norman, Welsh and Irish renditions."[7] Excellent scholarly accounts of the chain of English transmission are found in Simon Lavery's "The Story of Mary the Egyptian in Medieval England" and Jane Stevenson's "The Holy Sinner, The Life of Mary of Egypt" (both found in *The Legend of Mary of Egypt in Medieval Insular Hagiography*) and in Hugh Magennis's *The Old English Life of St. Mary of Egypt* (all cited in the bibliography). What follows is an abbreviated version of the literary/transmission history from the Middle East to the British Isles.

In his essay on Byzantine literature in *The Cambridge Medieval History,* Franz Dolger notes that "It was a genuine love of storytelling as well as a delight in miracles and the need to edify that produced the extensive and lively collection of Lives of the Saints which is one of the most characteristic achievements of Byzantine religious literature." He continues, "The lives and sayings of the monks who had retired into the desert to gain through their strivings special *charismata* or gifts of the Holy Spirit were of immense interest to contemporary readers."[8] Mary of Egypt's *vita*

---

7. Andrew P. Scheil, "Bodies and Boundaries in the Old English *Life of St. Mary of Egypt,*" *Neophilologus* 84 (2000): 138. I have found references to four Middle English redactions, three Anglo-Norman references in the 12th and 13th centuries, and four Welsh from the mid-13th to 14th centuries in addition to five Norse manuscripts from 1250 to 1445.

8. Franz Dolger, "Byzantine Literature," in *The Cambridge Medieval History*, vol. IV, part II, ed. J. M. Hussey (Cambridge: Cambridge University Press, 1967), 224, chap. 27. For more on Byzantine hagiography see 224–25.

is one of the most enduring of these. Mary of Egypt's death date has been variously assigned the years AD 421[9] and 430.[10] In scholarly literature she is usually referred to as a fifth-century saint. If we can trust the earliest texts, her story was told by Zossima to his brothers at the Jordan River monastery, then began to circulate not long after her death, in the late fifth century, certainly by the early sixth.

Several scholars suggest that the *Vita Pauli* by Saint Jerome (d. 420), the life of Paul of Thebes (traditionally the first Christian hermit, who died ca. 340), provided a model for the earliest lives of Mary of Egypt. Several scholars highlight the similarity between the *Vita Pauli* and Mary's life. Walsh, for example, referring to Sophronius's Greek life, which is apparently the first independent life of Mary, writes, "What is new in Sophronios . . . is that the anchorite is a woman."[11] Sophronius is often identified with the Patriarch of Jerusalem from 634 until his death in 638, but Dolger says his "identity with the Patriarch Sophronius of Jerusalem . . . is dubious." Sophronius had first been a monk in Egypt in a monastery near the Jordan, which may place him relatively near the events of Mary's life. Dolger goes on to say that Sophronius's "*Lives of John and Cyrus* and his *Mary the Egyptian* are presented in a highly rhetorical style and somewhat pedantically rhythmical prose."[12] Other scholars suggest Sophronius's narrative is a re-working of a story that first appeared in the "Life of Kyriakos" by Cyril of Scythopolis (ca. 560).[13] In a digression of some six hundred words in that work, Abba John encounters in a cave a solitary who had been a harpist in Jerusalem but who, as a result of scandal, had fled to the desert, where she had lived

9. E. D. Carter, "Mary of Egypt, St.," *New Catholic Encyclopedia* (Washington, DC: Catholic University Press, 1967), IX:387.

10. Heron, "Lioness," 23.

11. Walsh, "Ascetic Mother," 63.

12. Dolger, "Byzantine Literature," 224–25.

13. An English translation is found in R. M. Price, trans., *Cyril of Scythopolis: The Lives of the Monks of Palestine,* CS 114 (Kalamazoo, MI: Cistercian Publications, 1991). Mary's story is reflected in pages 256–57.

for eighteen years. She asks him to return again, and when he does, she is dead.[14] Sr. Benedicta Ward, SLG, includes Cyril of Scythopolis's story in her chapter on Mary in *Harlots of Desert*.[15]

Magennis writes that Mary's story came to the Latin West by means of Greek and Palestinian travelers.[16] The most widely known Latin life of Saint Mary of Egypt is that of Paul the Deacon (d. ca. 790).[17] Paul was a monk of Monte Cassino, a chronicler and scholar who was important in the development of early Medieval Latin and who for some years served Charlemagne. Paul's *vita* is a literary translation into Latin of Sophronius's Greek life. Paul describes himself as "the worthy deacon of the church at holy Naples," who "translated from the Greek language into Latin the most praiseworthy conversion . . . and the great repentance and very brave struggle of the worthy Mary of Egypt, how she completed the days of her life in the desert." He continues, "far be it from me that I should engage in falsification in the details of the holy narrative."[18] A complete English translation of the *"Life of St. Mary of Egypt* by Sophronius, bishop of Jerusalem, translated into Latin by Paul, deacon of the holy church of Naples," is also found in Ward's book.[19]

It is possible that knowledge of Mary of Egypt came to England via the Greek Archbishop of Canterbury, Theodore of Tarsus

14. Jane Stevenson, "The Holy Sinner: The Life of Mary of Egypt," in Poppe and Ross, *Legend of Mary*, 20–21.

15. Benedicta Ward, *Harlots of the Desert: A Study of Repentance in Early Monastic Sources,* CS 106 (Kalamazoo, MI: Cistercian Publications, 1987), 28–29.

16. Hugh Magennis, trans., *The Old English Life of St. Mary of Egypt* (Exeter: University of Exeter Press, 2002), 11.

17. The Latin text translated by Paul from the Greek of Sophronius appears in *Patrologiae cursus completus: series latina,* ed. J. P. Migne (Paris, 1844–1846), 73:671–90; *Bibliotheca Hagiographica Latina* (Brussels, 1901).

18. Quoted in Magennis, *Old English Life,* 59.

19. Ward, *Harlots of the Desert,* 35–56.

(602–690). Her story would also have been carried by continental monks to the British Isles and perhaps directly from Egypt to Ireland via monks.[20] The medieval period was one that Hildegard Tristram helpfully calls a time of "cultural interaccessibility," a period of trade, raiding, warfare, mobility, and multilingualism. Latin was the international language among many vernaculars from which there was translation from one to another. "Medieval cosmopolitanism," Tristram says, rested on the universal knowledge of Latin.[21] At any rate, Mary's feast day appears in Anglo-Saxon liturgical calendars, and the earliest vernacular account of Mary of Egypt in Old English is based on Paul's life, dated in the tenth or early eleventh century, and closely follows the Latin.[22] Simon Lavery's "The Story of Mary the Egyptian in Medieval England" provides a concise and comprehensive review of the many redactions of her story.[23]

The differences in the telling of Mary's story in the many versions and vernaculars in which we find it are due to the sources used, the time period in which they were written, and the locations of the translation. For example, Lavery points out that the Greco-Latin texts were made for court and monastic circles and reflect an austere style and avoid sensuality in telling the story.[24] The Old French versions present Mary of Egypt as a dangerous courtesan, and "the penitent is less active and interesting than the sinner."[25] The insular (British Isles, Ireland, Iceland) accounts reflect popular interest in miracle stories connected with saints'

20. See David Knowles, *Christian Monasticism* (New York: McGraw-Hill, 1969/1977), chaps. 1 and 2.

21. Tristram, Introduction, 2–8. She adds that "scholars who are competent in only one language and one area cannot possibly claim to have a true sense of the importance of the works they study" (12).

22. Magennis, *Old English Life,* 10–12, 43; Tristram, Introduction, 14.

23. Simon Lavery, "The Story of Mary the Egyptian in Medieval England," in Poppe and Ross, *Legend of Mary,* 113–48.

24. Lavery, "Story of Mary," 124, 132.

25. Lavery, "Story of Mary," 135.

tombs and miraculous conversions via the intercession of the Blessed Virgin Mary. They soften the austere, Byzantine story and focus on the Blessed Virgin's mediating role.[26] The basic narrative of Mary of Egypt was retained, but it was malleable. Its shape shifted to fit concerns of the age and place in which it was produced.

There is a very extensive scholarly literature on the versions of the life of Mary of Egypt in the British Isles and Ireland, where, as on the continent, she was a popular saint among monastics and in the general population. This very condensed account of the story's transmission suggests two primary things. First, there are historical and geographical connections among the life of Mary as it (probably) occurred, has been told, and was recorded by its first chroniclers. The written record of Mary of Egypt is ancient and unbroken from its origins into the medieval and early modern period. Second, from an early period there are multiple written lives, later in multiple languages. Something about the story of Mary of Egypt appealed to Christians across continents, societies, and languages. She survived the move from early Christianity in the Middle East into far-flung Byzantium in the East, and the medieval period in the West. Although her story is told from slightly different angles in different cultures and for different audiences, its appeal seems universal, in part because that appeal was both literary and theological. It is to those aspects of the written lives of Mary of Egypt that we now turn.

Literary Echoes, Antecedents, and Techniques

One reason Mary of Egypt's story endured was that it was such a *good* tale. But as Ward makes clear, "the story of Mary of Egypt is of deeper significance than simply a dramatic tale of lust turned into love. It is clearly packed with intricate symbols."[27] In fact Magennis points out that in most Old English saints' lives the

26. Lavery, "Story of Mary," 137.
27. Ward, *Harlots of the Desert,* 33.

symbolic is stressed rather than the temporal, and the importance of the story is what is "typified."[28] Some of this typology and symbolic material will be introduced later in this essay. Another reason that Mary's story caught on is that its writing reflected popular literary conventions and patterns in various times and places. From a practical standpoint, a new or surprising message is best presented in a familiar form. The old, old story may be more palatable in modern dress. Mary's story echoed desert narratives, journey stories, and moral parables as well as images and symbols known to its audience.

From its initial audience through those in the medieval period and beyond, Mary's narrative reflects two well-known structural patterns: the journey narrative and the story-within-a-story technique. Journey narratives hold fascination both for those who never leave home (certainly the majority of the tale's initial audiences) and for those who do and who in reading another's account recall the localities and challenges of their own travels. In an essay on early Christian women, after mentioning "Mary the Egyptian," Monique Alexandre notes, "The early Christians were fond of reading about pilgrimages"[29] and recalls the *Peregrinatio Silviae*, the pilgrimage of the nun Egeria to the Holy Land in the late fourth or early fifth century and her account of her travels, which provides important information on Christian liturgical practice and monasteries.[30]

Certainly in the medieval period some Europeans would have known Alexandria, Jerusalem, and the Jordan desert from pilgrimage

28. Hugh Magennis, "Conversion in Old English Saints' Lives," in *Essays on Anglo-Saxon and Related Themes in Memory of Lynne Grundy,* ed. Jane Roberts and Janet Nelson, King's College London Medieval Series 17 (London: King's College London Centre for Late Antique and Medieval Studies, 2000), 289.

29. Monique Alexandre, "Early Christian Women," in *A History of Women in the West: I. From Ancient Goddesses to Christian Saints*, ed. Pauline Schmitt Pantel (Cambridge, MA: The Belknap Press of Harvard University Press, 1992), 411.

30. See Egeria, *Diary of a Pilgrimage*, trans. George E. Gingras, Ancient Christian Writers 38 (New York: Newman Press, 1970).

or Crusade.[31] In biblical literature, the Exodus account of Moses and the Hebrews in the wilderness as well as the travels of Saint Paul in the Acts of the Apostles provided paradigms. Homer's *Odyssey* was and is the paradigmatic Greek journey story. Any number of medieval romances depict the travels of the hero, and Dante's *Divine Comedy* is a cosmic travel narrative. So Mary's external journeys from her home in Egypt to Alexandria to Jerusalem and into the desert beyond the Jordan (which, of course, depict her interior, spiritual pilgrimage) reflect a well-known journey motif that is also alluded to in Zossima's story as he travels to various monasteries on his own external/internal quest.

The coming together of the journeys of Mary and Zossima reflects another structural technique, that of a story-within-a-story and additionally *within* a travel narrative. It is the technique of Giovanni Boccaccio in *The Decameron* and Geoffrey Chaucer in *The Canterbury Tales*. In the traditional renderings of the story (from which my poems depart), Zossima's narrative frames Mary's, into which, though of primary interest, hers is inserted. Simon Lavery points out that this complex double structure allows the witness (Zossima) to preserve the solitary's (Mary) story.[32] The outer or external events are foils to the inner story of each character, and there is a network of contrasts between the two and within each character. For example, each story has two stages: city/desert (Mary) and monastery/desert (Zossima), geographical stages that mirror spiritual states, courtesan/penitent (Mary) and proud/humble (Zossima). The two stories intersect in the desert, which is for each character the locus of spiritual maturity. In effect, the story-within-a-story technique reflects a third literary device or structural principle: comparison and contrast.

---

31. In *Mystics and Zen Masters,* a collection of his essays, Thomas Merton's chapter "From Pilgrimage to Crusade" provides a helpful description of the two and the outcomes of each motivation for travel (New York: Farrar, Straus and Giroux, 1961/1987), 91–112.

32. Lavery, "Story of Mary," 128–30. My reading here relies upon Lavery's.

Within these well-known and frequently used macro-structural devices, the language of the telling would also have made the story accessible both in its diction and in what I shall call "metaphorical shorthand." In their translation of Mary's story from a Slavonic version into English, Srs. Katherine and Thekla note that the "language is unemphatic, conventionally pious in tone, and with the conversational, even intimate note, of imparting a well-known and much-loved story."[33] Mary of Egypt's story was accessible because its language was not the language of the court or the monastic scholar, but of the common person, and it also reflected a symbolic, metaphorical shorthand that was widely understood.

In a very helpful essay, "*Imago Dei*: Genre, Symbolism, and Anglo-Saxon Hagiography," Thomas Hill explains that not only did the literary *vita* imitate secular literary forms, but all medieval vernacular hagiography was dependent upon Christian prototypes and exemplars.[34] Literary study calls this typology or figuration. Typology, from the Greek *typos*, impression or model, and the Latin *typus*, image, employs individuals, places, or actions to suggest certain typical characteristics, so that, for example, a character in a story is representative of a class or group of people rather than a single individual, or a specific place is suggestive of a psychological or moral category. A person or thing prefigures or stands for a wider category. Figuration refers to a person, place, thing, or action's serving as representative of something beyond or larger than itself, expressing one thing in terms of something else (which, of course, is a characteristic of poetry, and might be said of religious and all metaphorical language).

Hill's essay suggests that hagiography (like iconography) works by means of figuration or typology and is "a mode of understanding

---

33. Sr. Katherine and Sr. Thekla, *St. Andrew of Crete*, 21.

34. Thomas D. Hill, "*Imago Dei*: Genre, Symbolism, and Anglo-Saxon Hagiography," in *Holy Men and Holy Women: Old English Prose Saints' Lives and Their Contexts*, ed. Paul E. Szarmach, SUNY Series in Medieval Studies (Albany: State University of New York Press, 1996), 38, 35.

Christian history" and "an integral aspect of biblical thought."[35]
Christian hearers were familiar with this form. They knew biblical
texts like Hosea, whose family situation is an emblem of God's
relationship with humanity, or the Song of Songs/Song of Solomon,
which was really about the soul's longing for God. Thus, the story
of a saint like Mary of Egypt is historical, but not history, in part
because of its figural patterns. People read or heard the events in
Mary's life and recognized what they meant or were figures for.
In what Hill calls an "emblematic narrative," inner experiences
are reflected by external events in that narrative, just as metaphors
concerning the religious truth are expressed in narrative form.[36]
These narratives combine reality (or history) and its symbolic (or
transcendent) meaning.

This process is seen in three of the many possible examples of
metaphorical shorthand from the life of Mary of Egypt: the loca-
tion of the desert, the character of the harlot or prostitute (though
as the poem "Mary Explains Why" on page 19 suggests, she was
not exactly either), and the appearance of the lion.

The Desert

The desert is one of the oldest and most pervasive "types" in
biblical and Christian tradition. The desert (*eremos* in Greek),
which wasn't technically a geographical term but means a lonely,
deserted, desolate, or solitary place, thus a dangerous place, was
associated with Moses and the Hebrews' forty-year sojourn in the
Sinai and the miraculous food (manna); with Elijah, his escape
from Ahab and Jezebel, miraculous feeding, and God as fire and "a
sound of sheer silence" (1 Kgs 29:12, NRSV); with the forerunner,
John the Baptist; and with the desert temptations of Jesus.[37] In

---

35. Hill, "*Imago Dei,*" 43, 44.

36. Hill, "*Imago Dei,*" 45.

37. For more on the desert, see "The Wilderness and the Desert/Chaos and
Comfort," in my study *The Spiritual Landscape of Mark* (Collegeville, MN:
Liturgical Press, 2008), 1–14, chap. 1.

the Bible the desert is the place of encounter with God and, as a result, of spiritual transformation. One could multiply examples. The point is that the desert is the place to which people flee, meet, and are sustained and transformed by encounter with God.

Mary of Egypt's story is to be heard in light of all that and, especially, of the lives of the fourth-century Desert Christians, who, in the words of the American Cistercian monk, Thomas Merton, went to the desert to seek "their own, true self, in Christ". . . "they had come into the desert to be themselves . . . and to forget a world that divided them from themselves."[38] In *Sacred Fictions: Holy Women and Hagiography in Late Antiquity,* Lynda L. Coon puts the matter succinctly and dramatically: the desert is "a sacred terrain, where emaciated hermits recreate Christ's passion through ascetic practices," and where female ascetics "atone for the sorrowful life of the postlapsarian Eve."[39]

Here the structure of the travel narrative and the typology of the desert come powerfully together. Mary's journey took her to Jerusalem where, as Judith Weiss notes, her prayer to the Blessed Virgin Mary uses the language of travel to express spiritual change.[40] Crossing the Jordan River symbolizes a change in her state (as, indeed, does crossing the Jordan in several biblical narratives). Fallen Mary entered the desert, the place of danger and encounter with God, and was spiritually uplifted and changed. It is reminiscent of what the little prince says in that most metaphorical children's book, *The Little Prince*: " 'What makes the desert beautiful,' said the little prince, 'is that somewhere it hides a well.' "[41]

38. Thomas Merton, *The Wisdom of the Desert* (New York: New Directions, 1960), 5, 23.

39. Lynda L. Coon, *Sacred Fictions: Holy Women and Hagiography in Late Antiquity* (Philadelphia: University of Pennsylvania Press, 1997), 71, 72.

40. Judith Weiss, "The Metaphor of Madness in the Anglo-Norman Lives of St. Mary the Egyptian," in Poppe and Ross, *Legend of Mary,* 168.

41. Antoine de Saint-Exupery, *The Little Prince* (New York: Harcourt, Brace, & World, 1943), 75.

As Stevenson astutely remarks, one can live in the desert so long as she is prepared to merge into it.[42]

The desert setting in Mary's story is rich and complex. It adds the delightful frisson of danger or dis-ease to her story because the desert is a complex symbol. *The Penguin Dictionary of Symbols* provides a succinct summary of this point: "the desert, without God, is barrenness: with God it is fruitfulness, but fruitfulness due to God alone. The desert displays the supremacy of grace. In the spiritual order nothing exists without it: all exists through it and through it alone."[43] The "metaphorical shorthand" of the desert is related to that of the prostitute or harlot. Mary of Egypt lived like a desert animal and became an angel. Mary of Egypt goes to the desert and receives "the supremacy of grace."

The Harlot

Jane Stevenson reminds us that in Late Antiquity Egyptian prostitutes were considered exotic and dangerous women.[44] That the exotic and dangerous could become the familiar and saintly was part of the appeal of Mary's story. In earlier ages, readers or hearers of Saint Mary of Egypt's story would have known she was not the only woman who began as a harlot and became a saint. Although the evidence for it rests on a mis-reading of gospel texts, Mary Magdalene (the "apostle to the apostles" in the Orthodox church) was (and, alas, remains) the paradigm of the bad-girl-become-good.[45] As was mentioned in the introduction, she and Mary of

42. Stevenson, "Holy Sinner," 39.

43. Jean Chevalier and Alain Gheerbrant, *The Penguin Dictionary of Symbols*, trans. John Buchanan-Brown (London: Penguin Books, 1994), 286.

44. Stevenson, "Holy Sinner," 22.

45. I am not the only biblical scholar who has rehabilitated Mary of Magdala. See Ann Graham Brock, *Mary Magdalene, The First Apostle* (Cambridge, MA: Harvard University Press, 2003); Esther de Boer, *Mary Magdalene: Beyond the Myth* (Harrisburg, PA: Trinity Press International, 1996); Holly E. Hearon, *The Mary Magdalene Tradition* (Collegeville, MN: Liturgical Press, 2004); Ingrid Maisch, *Mary Magdalene: The Image of a Woman through the Centuries*

Egypt are still inaccurately conflated. There are Byzantine-era lives of harlots who became ascetics—for example, Pelagia and Thais. In addition to Mary of Magdala, Ward's *Harlots of the Desert: A Study of Repentance in Early Monastic Sources* includes Saint Mary of Egypt, Pelagia, Thais, and Maria the Niece of Abraham.

Then there is the life of the undoubtedly historical Theodora, who became the wife of the influential Emperor Justinian I (ca. 483–565). Reputedly having lived "a very dissolute life in her earlier years,"[46] Theodora married Justinian in 523 and was crowned co-regnant empress in 527. A woman of learning and intellect, she actively entered the theological discussions of the time in favor of Monophysite Christians (who revere her as a saint). Said to have been a moral reformer, she died in 548 after a respectable married life. She is another example of the sexual sinner become exemplary Christian, which so appealed (and appeals?) to popular imagination (as does the trope of the "good-hearted prostitute"). There are a mosaic portrait of Theodora in the Church of San Vitale in Ravenna, Italy, several modern scholarly biographies and studies of her life, and a number of literary and artistic portrayals.

Stories like these reflected the Greco-Roman medical theory that women were more lustful than men and, therefore, must of course be under male control. Stevenson points out that late antiquity had high standards for women's behavior and that, effectively, certain people, such as prostitutes, were beneath the law and had no legal existence. Part of the jolt of the story of Mary of Egypt

(Collegeville, MN: Liturgical Press, 1998); Mary R. Thompson, *Mary of Magdala, Apostle and Leader* (New York: Paulist Press, 1995); and chapter 2 of Benedicta Ward's *Harlots of the Desert*. Also of interest is the undated, but probably late-first- or early-second-century "Gospel of Mary," in *The Complete Gospels,* ed. Robert J. Miller (San Francisco: HarperSanFrancisco, 1994), analyzed by Karen L. King, "The Gospel of Mary Magdalene," in Elisabeth Schussler Fiorenza, *Searching the Scriptures: A Feminist Commentary* (New York: Crossroad, 1994), chap. 32.

46. F. L. Cross and E. A. Livingstone, *The Oxford Dictionary of the Christian Church* (Oxford: Oxford University Press, 1997), 1598, col. 2.

to the original audiences is that Fr. Zossima "is humble and acute enough to see that a discarded scrap of human garbage might be both a great lady, and a vehicle for great truths."[47] Mary's story symbolizes an ancient archetype and a Christian conviction: that evil can turn to good, that sinners can not only repent but become sources of spiritual wisdom, and that, therefore, it is best to suspend judgment of others.

Mary of Egypt's story reflects traditional gender expectations by means of the conventional, literary theme of the harlot as sinful but redeemable. Lynda Coon correctly observes that through its mortification, the body of the harlot not only reverses Eve's fall, but promotes the cult of the *Theotokos* (who guided her to and in the desert) and reinforces hope that redemption is possible for loathsome sinners.[48] Additionally, earlier generations of readers/hearers "saw the image of the prostitute as a way of describing inner experience."[49] Her life was a *psychomachia,* an exterior presentation of an interior journey. As was noted above, the exterior narrative mirrors the interior journey. Mary of Egypt incarnates the typology of the repentant sinner, which reflects the grace of the desert's typology.[50] And the desert is the abode of the lion.

---

47. Stevenson, "Holy Sinner," 28.

48. Coon, *Sacred Fictions,* 91, 94.

49. Ward, *Harlots of the Desert,* 33.

50. See Hugh Magennis, "St. Mary of Egypt and Aelfric: Unlikely Bedfellows in Cotton Julius E.vii?" in Poppe and Ross, *Legend of Mary,* 99–112. Magennis points out that by renouncing sexuality and dedicating themselves to chastity, women freed themselves from male control in a "holy subversion of social expectations" (107). The medieval church, he points out, was uncomfortable with independent spirituality, especially that of women in a male hierarchy. Female saints shouldn't infringe on male authority: "Mary of Egypt presents a radical contrast with the images of female sanctity cultivated by Aelfric," who admires her for having overcome enslavement to sexual appetite (109). But the story is one of a non-virgin, independent of church structures, who teaches a monk and priest, a woman who presented "a radically alternative spiritual idea" (111). The archetypal aspect of her story (sinner to saint) was edifying to everybody. One can only imagine how encouraging it must have been to women.

The Lion

The use of animals as ideological symbols has a long history in both literature and painting and endures today, for example, in political cartoons in which the bear represents Russia or the bulldog England. One thinks of the beasts in apocalyptic biblical books like Ezekiel and the Revelation to John, of the dove as a universal symbol of peace, the fox as sly wisdom, and the convoluted image of the serpent as evil, wisdom, healing, and life force. The English might think of the "Queen's Beasts," lion, griffin, and dragon, or Americans the eagle. Especially in view of modern, dramatic presentations of *The Lion King*, we hardly need *The Penguin Dictionary of Symbols* to tell us that the lion is the "King of the Beasts." But it does remind us that "the lion is burdened with the virtues and defects which are inherent in its status."[51] He may embody power, wisdom, and justice, but this can lead to pride, a dangerous sin, indeed, as Zossima's story attests.

In early manuscripts of Mary of Egypt's story, when the lion appears to help Zossima bury Mary's body, it was already the carrier of many symbolic ideas. Biblically we might think first of Daniel and his friends in the lion's den. Certainly the psalmist uses the figure of the lion to represent sudden death in Psalm 22:21 ("Save me from the mouth of the lion"), and 2 Timothy 4:17 speaks of deliverance from enemies: "I was rescued from the lion's mouth." In Psalm 91 we read, "Because you have made the Lord . . . your refuge . . . you will tread on the lion and adder: the young lion . . . you will trample under foot" (Ps 91:9, 13). Proverbs 28:1 describes the righteous person as "bold as a lion," an idea perhaps behind 1 Peter 5:8, in which, "like a roaring lion your adversary the devil prowls around, looking for someone to devour."

When the lion does something other than feed on smaller creatures, people sit up and take notice. The prophet Isaiah's vision of the peaceable kingdom in Isaiah 11:6-7 reverses the usual biblical image of the lion as predator: "the leopard shall lie down with the kid, and the calf and the lion and the fatling together," and "the lion

---

51. *Penguin Dictionary of Symbols,* 611.

shall eat straw like the ox"; in other words, the lion naps with what normally would have been his dinner and becomes a vegetarian, a ruminant like a cow. When a lion appears at the end of Mary's story, the hearer might expect it to gobble up Zossima. But they meet by a saint's corpse in the desert of grace, and the lion assists at the burial. This unusual and exciting reversal in a lion's behavior in the original telling of Mary's story has precedents in the lives of the desert Christians of the fourth century and of other early saints of the church. A few examples follow.

When a desert monk near the Jordan went into a cave to escape the heat, he found a lion already in residence and gnashing its teeth. When the monk suggested that there was room for them both, the lion left. Another lion story set near the Jordan River is of Abbot Gerasimus, who removed a thorn from a lion's paw, and in gratitude the lion served him like a loyal dog until the monk died. Saint Jerome greeted a lion that wandered into the monastery and treated its thorn-wounded paw, and it became an animal servant of the monastery. And there are other similar stories about lions and saints' relationships with other animals.[52] Proximity to saints seems to tame the King of the Beasts (perhaps a figuration of taming sexual passion).

Earlier readers and hearers of the story of Mary of Egypt would have been likely to remember the biblical lion images from hearing them in the monastic Offices (especially the Psalms) or church liturgy. As well as biblical material, Christology was taught to the illiterate through pictures. Medieval peasants might have known the image of "the Lion of the tribe of Judah, the Root of David," used in the Revelation to John to allude to the Christ (or at least to the heavenly figure who is to open the book and loose the seven seals, Rev 5:5). Just as a place (the desert) and a person (a harlot) had resonance for those who encountered Mary's story, the lion

52. A particularly charming collection is English scholar Helen Waddell's *Beasts and Saints* (London: Constable and Company, 1934/1953), illustrated with woodcuts by Robert Gibbings.

would have been an important symbolic figure. Especially in the Eastern church where the lion is a symbol of Christ, Christians would have understood why it was a lion that made Zossima's final work possible.[53]

These images—desert, harlot, lion—would have carried a weight of significance that deepened meaning for the recipients of Mary's story. For many, if not most of them, the tale would originally have been heard against the backdrop of monastic life and its virtues and vices. In the Eastern church, Mary of Egypt's story was monastic. But as Walsh reminds us, "The story became enormously popular in the late middle ages in Western Europe, but a change had occurred in the emphasis. The tale was cast off from its monastic moorings." Still, Walsh correctly indicates that "not understanding the monastic elements of this story . . . one can miss its significance."[54] A well-constructed, allusively literary, and engaging tale, its origin was monastic, and its significance was (and is) theological, and it is to that aspect of the narrative that we now turn.

Theological Interest

First heard and preserved in monastic settings, Walsh explains, Mary of Egypt's story was first understood "strictly as a monastic document, written not to convert or to edify the masses but to teach monastics true humility."[55] Stevenson aptly calls it "a glittering mosaic of monastic spirituality."[56] The tenth-century Latin manuscripts rendered into Old English celebrate "a monastic spirituality that is rigorously ascetic and contemplative."[57]

---

53. David G. R. Keller, *Oasis of Wisdom (The Worlds of the Desert Fathers and Mothers)* (Collegeville, MN: Liturgical Press, 2005), 153.

54. Walsh, "Ascetic Mother," 68.

55. Walsh, "Ascetic Mother," 60.

56. Stevenson, "Holy Sinner," 35. I observe that scholars who divorce the story from its monastic origins tend to misread it.

57. Tristram, Introduction, 14.

It reflects theological and spiritual ideas that were (and are) central to the concerns of all who heard it, and, as the manuscript history attests, it became a widely popular story for the edification of a more general audience.

Although as Ward indicates they certainly *did so*, monks were not the only Christians who saw themselves "in need of mercy, as the penitent, as the sinner."[58] While the original intent of Mary's story may not have been catechetical, "to edify the masses," earlier generations of those "masses" were keenly aware that they, too, "have sinned and fall short of the glory of God" (Rom 3:23), and so "the complex of ideas connected with *penthos*—compunction—conversion" applied to them too.[59] It encouraged Christians to understand that the grace received by the great sinner Mary of Egypt and the prideful monk Zossima was available to them as well. To borrow a turn of phrase from Srs. Katherine and Thekla, Mary's story offered "the integration of the monastic aim into the every-day life of every one of the Faithful."[60] As Maria Kouli writes in the introduction to her translation of Mary's life, "if such a licentious woman could find forgiveness, surely ordinary sinners could hope for salvation."[61] The journey from sin to conversion, and the penitence that formed profound humility in the monk, was a journey for all Christians, who were aided and strengthened by the Eucharist and the Blessed Virgin Mary's intercession.

In practice, continental versions of Mary's story served as "hortatory *exempla* for . . . spiritual pilgrimage through the wilderness of the world."[62] Mary's life reflected orthodox teaching about the theology of penitence, conversion, humility, and the Blessed Virgin Mary, whose cult flourished during the period when Mary

---

58. Ward, *Harlots of the Desert,* 33.

59. Ronald Pepin and Hugh Feiss, trans., *Saint Mary of Egypt: Three Medieval Lives in Verse,* CS 209 (Kalamazoo, MI: Cistercian Publications, 2005), ix.

60. Sr. Katherine and Sr. Thekla, *St. Andrew of Crete,* 23.

61. Maria Kouli, trans., "Life of St. Mary of Egypt," in Talbot, *Holy Women,* 65.

62. Tristram, Introduction, 15.

of Egypt's story was most popular. That the Egyptian's was an entertaining story provided the spoon full of sugar that made the theological medicine go down. It is difficult to decide how to order these theological ideas, particularly those of penitence and conversion. The order that follows is from the narrative of Mary of Egypt's life: Mary's *conversion* and the *Blessed Virgin Mary's* critical role therein preceded the Egyptian's *penitence,* which is followed by her and Zossima's *humility.* Although it is certainly true that Zossima, too, is "converted," what follows focuses on Mary's conversion and re-introduces Zossima's story in a later section of this essay.

Conversion

A brief reminder of etymology helps to clarify what *conversion* entails. *Conversion* as used here reflects the Greek New Testament's word *metanoia,* a composite of *meta,* meaning "with," and the verb *noeo,* "to understand" or "to perceive." Usually translated "repent" or "change of heart" or "turn from sin," *metanoia* means to live with understanding, to perceive what *really is* the truth of things. *Conversion,* from the Latin *convertere,* with the root word *vertere,* "to turn," suggests turning away from one thing to something else, *being* transformed in some way. Conversion in Mary's story results from her perception of her true state and her turning toward something or Someone else.

William James's classic discussion of conversion in chapter nine of *The Varieties of Religious Experience* (1906) is still one of the most helpful. James writes that to be "converted" is "the process, gradual or sudden, by which a self hitherto divided, and consciously wrong, inferior and unhappy, becomes unified and consciously right superior and happy, in consequence of its firmer hold upon religious realities."[63] James observes two basic forms of conversion: the volitional, which is conscious, voluntary, and

63. William James, *The Varieties of Religious Experience* (New York: Collier Books, 1961, 1974), 160.

gradual, and that of self-surrender, which is unconscious and sudden.[64] The candidate for conversion is aware of sin to be left behind and a positive ideal to be appropriated.[65] The "proof" of conversion is that the life of the converted is transformed, not *how it happens* but *what is attained*, especially the sense of higher control and the state of assurance that all is ultimately well.[66]

James's template of self-surrender almost perfectly matches the narrative of Mary's life. Before conversion, hers was not a state of internal moral chaos, and those who first recorded the life were not interested in the psychology from which it may have arisen. Mary rejected good parents. She was nothing short of lascivious as she traveled to the city of Alexandria, where she enjoyed her sinfulness. For a time. Though presented as a stage in her lascivious life, Mary arrives in Jerusalem "weary, worn, and sad."[67] Her inability to enter the Church of the Holy Sepulcher/Resurrection symbolizes her own rejection of the Life it celebrates. The heart and spatial center of Mary of Egypt's story is her sudden conversion by means of and under the patronage of the Mother of Jesus (who is a shadowy but major character in the remainder of the story). Confronted with absolute and perfect purity, Mary of Egypt sees herself as she is. She gazes at the icon of the Blessed Virgin Mary and sees the inverse image of herself.

In *We, the Ordinary People of the Streets,* French Catholic Madeleine Delbrel writes, "Conversion is a decisive moment in which we turn ourselves away from what we know about ourselves so that, face to face with God, God can tell us what he thinks of our life and what he wants to do with it."[68] Gazing into the face of the Blessed Virgin Mary, Mary of Egypt sees the face of God

---

64. James, *Varieties,* 172.

65. James, *Varieties,* 174.

66. James, *Varieties*, 196. Italics in the original.

67. From the hymn "I heard the voice of Jesus say," Horatius Bonar, 1846.

68. Madeleine Delbrel, *We, The Ordinary People of the Streets* (Grand Rapids: Eerdmans, 2000), 264.

and is "totally bedazzled."[69] In one Old English version of her life she says of the event, "a knowledge of salvation touched my mind and the eyes of my heart."[70] The validity of this conversion is measured (as it is in all conversions) in the manifest change in the character, thought, and mode of life of Mary of Egypt. This aspect of conversion is not "once and for all," but "on going" and volitional. More will be said about that when penitence is considered.

In his essay "Conversion in Old English Saints' Lives," Magennis highlights the prevalence of this theme in the writings, noting, "For these writers conversion is normally something that saints do to other people."[71] In these narratives conversion happens by means of idealized figures of superhuman virtue who don't themselves need converting, and it is a mark of their sanctity that they bring others to God. There is a quality of timelessness or of being out of the realm of ordinary time that accompanies these saint-initiated conversions.[72] The influence of the Blessed Virgin on Mary's conversion conforms to this pattern. Our Lady is not only the initiator of the conversion, but as Egyptian Mary tells her story to Zossima, Our Lady is also her patroness and protector in her early temptations in the desert.

The Blessed Virgin Mary

Although Mary the mother of Jesus is mentioned infrequently in early patristic writing, and usually in connection with Eve, by the time of Mary of Egypt she had become a focus of popular devotion and of considerable theological interest. The Council of Ephesus in 431 (about the time Mary of Egypt died) officially sanctioned

---

69. Delbrel, *We,* 265.

70. Quoted in Magennis, "Conversion in Old English Saints' Lives," 302. The writer of the Ephesians letter, 1:18, prays that "the eyes of your heart" will be "enlightened."

71. Magennis, "Conversion," 287.

72. I am paraphrasing Magennis, "Conversion," 287–88.

the Blessed Virgin's title *Theotokos*, literally "God bearer," the one who gave birth to God, a designation upheld at Chalcedon in 451. Scholars suggest that the term was used in Alexandria as early as Origen (d. ca. 254) and was common by the fourth century. It was Cyril of Alexandria who promoted the title at the Council of Ephesus. At the very least, there are intriguing geographical and chronological overlaps between the theology of Mary of Nazareth and the life of Mary of Egypt.

By her own admission, Mary of Egypt's sudden conversion occurs when, after being denied entrance into the church to venerate Christ's cross, she comes face-to-face with an icon of the Blessed Virgin Mary. "Gazing directly into her eyes," Mary of Egypt addresses her as "Virgin and Lady" and "ever-immaculate Virgin," admits that she herself is defiled, and says, "Receive my confession, and give me leave to enter the church." She continues, "When I had said this, with burning faith, as if receiving some assurance from some sure source, and trusting in the mercy of the heart of the Mother of God, I . . . mingled with those who were going in."[73] The Blessed Virgin Mary is the agent (though not the origin) of the conversion of the Egyptian harlot, whose prayer to her was immediately answered.

The Oxford Dictionary of the Christian Church affirms that "Belief in the efficacy of Mary's intercession and hence direct prayers to her is prob. very old. It is attested in a Greek form of the well-known prayer 'Sub tuum praesidium' found in a papyrus dating from the late 3rd to early 4th cent."[74] After the Council of Ephesus, Mary's name and title appear in service books and liturgical prayers. In the Western church Thomas Aquinas (d. 1274) clarified her position by means of the term *hyperdulia* (*huper*, "more than," and *douleia*, from the noun *doulos*, "slave," "servitude," or "veneration"). Mary is to be venerated because she was the *Theotokos*, the Bearer or Mother of God, but not "worshiped"

---

73. Ward's translation of Paul the Deacon's Latin in *Harlots of the Desert*, 47.
74. Cross and Livingstone, *Oxford Dictionary*, 1048, col. 1.

(*latria*) as was her Son. Andrew Louth correctly notes, "In Catholic and Orthodox Mariology the dogmas of our Lady are derived out of, and retain their significance in the context of, Christology. They disclose Mary's role in the mystery of redemption."[75]

Both that role and mystery are preeminent in the narrative of Mary of Egypt, a narrative that both gives substance to Mariology and demonstrates popular piety regarding the Blessed Virgin. Stevenson points out that devotion to the Blessed Virgin Mary characterized the spirituality of the Palestinian monks in both the veneration of her icons and belief in the efficacy of her intercession.[76] Efthalia Walsh is not the only scholar who notes "that the Theotokos was the one who freed Mary, suggests a possible female-saved-by-female motif,"[77] a matter to be revisited in the section of this essay on contemporary interest in Mary of Egypt—who certainly "departs from stereotypical portrayals of female piety."[78]

The point here is that the critical role played by the Virgin Mary, to whom Mary of Egypt addresses her prayer of confession before her conversion and her prayers for help in the temptations of her early years in the desert,[79] not only reflects orthodox theology about our Lady, but appealed to popular devotion to her, not only at the time of the original story, but well beyond it in Christian history. It is not surprising that Mary of Egypt's story is well attested in the medieval period when devotion to her patroness the

75. Andrew Louth, *Mary and the Mystery of Incarnation* (Fairacres, Oxford: SLG Press, 1977, 2002), 22.

76. Stevenson, "Holy Sinner," 33.

77. Walsh, "Ascetic Mother," 67.

78. Coon, *Sacred Fictions,* 84.

79. In response to Zossima's question about how she persevered in the desert, Mary responds, "In imagination, I would come before the picture of the Holy Mother of God . . . and implore her to chase from me those thoughts which were afflicting my most wretched soul. . . . [M]y helper the Mother of God has been with me, and she directed me in all things" (from the translation in Ward, *Harlots of the Desert,* 50).

Theotokos was ubiquitous in every place and at every level of Christian society. Louth explains, "Mary is not independent. . . . She is the Mother of God, deriving her meaning and significance from our Lord; and she is, herself, a woman, one of us."[80] He notes that "Mary stands beside me as one who helps me to contemplate the wonder of God disclosed in the Incarnation."[81] Saint Ambrose may be correct in calling the Blessed Virgin Mary a type of the church, but her enduring place in popular piety is her role as Universal Mother to whom monks, Mary of Egypt, and sinners "flee for refuge." For Mary of Egypt and for other Christians, the *Theotokos* is the human face and flesh of the incarnation. The common condition of sin (to which Mary of Egypt confessed to the *Theotokos*) made penitence another important theological focus of the narrative.

Penitence/Repentance

In considering the theological importance of Mary of Egypt's narrative it could be argued that its primary theological contribution is in its depiction of repentance. In *Harlots of the Desert* Ward subtitles her chapter on Mary "The Liturgical Icon of Repentance."[82] In my essay's organization, the matter of penitence could have preceded or immediately followed that of conversion. However, in Mary's story, her removal to the desert across the Jordan and her life of ascetic penitence there *follows* her dramatic conversion in Jerusalem. In the monastic tradition that preserved her story, conversion is not a shattering one-off event, but the on-going challenge to conform a human life to the model of the Lord Jesus.

In his book *The Monastic Journey,* Thomas Merton opens his chapter on conversion of life with the words, "The vow of *conversatio morum* (conversion of life) is the essential monastic vow."[83]

80. Louth, *Mary,* 22.

81. Louth, *Mary,* 23.

82. Ward, *Harlots of the Desert,* 26–56.

83. Thomas Merton, *The Monastic Journey*, ed. Br. Patrick Hart (Kansas City: Sheed, Andrews and McMeel, 1977), 107.

He continues, "The way of monastic *conversatio* is to renounce all and offer oneself totally to God."[84] This is a continual process; one chooses it moment to moment and day by day. For some it is an on-going penitence, like Mary of Egypt's forty-seven years in the desert. If, as Merton suggests, "the monk is one who has chosen not to live among men of the world and according to their standards,"[85] Mary of Egypt became a monk in this sense, and Zossima, who was a monk in the more conventional and institutional sense, recognized her perfection as such.

Without turning this discussion into a Penitential (like the books that arose in about the sixth century in the Celtic church, which listed sins and their appropriate penances), it may be helpful in thinking about the *metanoia* of Mary and of Zossima to consider a series of terms related to conversion. *Compunction* (from the Latin root *punctio*, "to prick hard," from which we get the word *puncture*) is the anxiety that arises from the awareness of guilt, the "painful sting of conscience." From it *penitence* (from the Latin root *penitentia*), realization of and regret for misdeeds, failures, or sins, may follow. *Repentance* adds to penitence the resolve to change. One regrets sin and resolves not to repeat it or to continue in it. Indeed, Srs. Katherine and Thekla suggest, "We do not know the value of any thought or action. And, so, we repent."[86] *Contrition* (related to the Latin *conterere*, "to rub together, grind," or "bruise") has been described as the sorrowful regret of true repentance. It is related to *remorse* (Latin *re-* "again" and *mordere-* "to bite"), prolonged self-reproach for past wrongs, torturing, unresolved guilt, especially perhaps for past mistakes the consequences of which cannot be remedied.

The experiences of life are not as clear cut as the Latin roots of English words. The lives of Mary and of Zossima do not proceed in orderly fashion from compunction to penitence and repentance/ contrition to happily ever after (at least not immediately). But

---

84. Merton, *Monastic Journey,* 111.
85. Merton, *Monastic Journey,* 117.
86. Sr. Katherine and Sr. Thekla, *St. Andrew of Crete,* 24.

in the narrative both characters exhibit characteristics of each experience. And each is spared the psychologically crippling experience of remorse by means of confession: Mary of Egypt to the Blessed Virgin Mary and to Zossima, and Zossima to himself in self-awareness and (eventually) to his brothers in relating the story of his encounters with Mary and their effect on him. In her reflection on Mary of Egypt in *The Cloister Walk*, Kathleen Norris writes, "Repentance is not a popular word these days, but I believe that any of us recognize it when it strikes us in the gut. Repentance is coming to our senses, seeing, suddenly, what we've done that we might not have done. . . . Repentance is valuable because it opens in us the idea of change."[87] Change can be for the better, which is the point of *conversatio morum* in the monastic life.

In the Mary of Egypt story (as in many classic conversion tales), a noteworthy feature of the process is tears. Stevenson has noted the "lachrymoseness of the narrative," the high value it places on tears as indicative of the movement toward God (which she terms "compunction").[88] Carmel Posa concurs: "Closely tied to this theme of repentance is the attitude of compunction or *penthos*, the gift of tears. Tears flow copiously from the eyes of both Mary and Zossima and flood the pages of this tale with the overwhelming sense of repentance and the need for mercy. Indeed, tears signify repentance." She continues, "These tears indicate a growing awareness of one's sinful condition before a merciful God." Posa's analysis concludes, "The 'Godly sorrow' of *penthos* is the source of joy and thanksgiving."[89]

It is also, as Walsh points out, one of "a whole series of events in the Mary story [that] have special monastic meanings. The weeping and grieving in front of the icon is an important sign; cry-

87. Kathleen Norris, *The Cloister Walk* (New York: Riverhead Books, 1996), 165–66.

88. Stevenson, "Holy Sinner," 37.

89. Carmel M. Posa, "Mary and Zossima: Icons of Mutuality in the Spiritual Journey," *Tjurunga* 57 (1999): 19.

ing, tears, seeing light are stages in the process of repentance."[90] From the stance of a scholar of depth psychology, Dr. Pia Sophia Chaudhari writes about Mary of Egypt, noting that in the clinical setting, when people begin to weep, it signals that they "turn a good corner and suddenly see the darknesses of the past thrown into relief by the clear light of the present. Tears herald the mourning required, of who we have been and where we have been, before the new which has arrived can take root and grow."[91] When Mary weeps before the Virgin's icon or Zossima weeps at the feet of Mary (thereby reversing the gender roles in Luke 7:38), it is a positive sign of their on-going conversion, the *conversatio morum* of monastic life, the desired end of which is humility.

Humility

If repentance isn't currently a popular subject for theology (and it isn't because it assumes fallibility and sin, both *anathema* in a "we're all O.K." world), humility loses the popularity contest hands down. But humility is the fruit of true contrition, penitence, and repentance. One recognizes how far one has fallen, and yet has been mercifully, like the good thief in Luke 23:43, lifted up by being forgiven. The result is humility, a primary consideration of monastic life.

The sayings of the desert Christians of the fourth century are full of teachings on humility. For example, John the Dwarf said, "Humility and the fear of God are above all virtues."[92] John of the Thebaid said, "First of all the monk must gain humility."[93]

90. Walsh, "Ascetic Mother," 64.

91. Pia Sophia Chaudhari, "Depth Psychology and the Courage of St. Mary of Egypt," *Public Orthodoxy* website. For full reference please see bibliography.

92. Benedicta Ward, *The Desert Christian: The Sayings of the Desert Fathers* (New York: Macmillan, 1975), 90. There are some thirty-six references to humility in this volume.

93. Ward, *Desert Christian,* 106.

Abba Or said, "The crown of the monk is humility."[94] One could multiply examples. The point is that humility was the life and breath of monasticism at the time of Mary of Egypt and Zossima. As was noted previously, Walsh reminds us that Mary's story was "written not to convert or edify the masses but to teach monastics true humility."[95] Roughly a century later (ca. 540), The Rule of Saint Benedict, one of monasticism's foundational documents, in chapter six lists the twelve steps of humility.[96]

Theologically and practically, it is important to understand that being humble is not being a human doormat or exhibiting false modesty about one's gifts and strengths. It is about submissiveness to God after the model of Jesus Christ, about human-ness, and self-knowledge. Perhaps the oldest text in the New Testament is the "Christ hymn" that Paul quotes in Philippians 2:6-11. The *peripeteia* of the hymn, the reversal of the fortunes of its "hero," occurs not because the Christ "was in the form of God" (2:6, as he was), but comes *after* "he humbled himself and became obedient to the point of death—even death on a cross" (2:8): "*Therefore* God also highly exalted him" (2:9, italics mine). The writers of the Synoptic Gospels (Matthew, Mark, and Luke) seldom record what Jesus says about himself, probably because he seldom says anything about himself. A notable exception appears in Matthew 11:28; Jesus says, "I am gentle and humble of heart." In Jesus' world nobody wanted to be humble, because humility (*tapeinos,* "humble, lowly, of humble circumstance") was a slave virtue. The humility of Christians was (and is) counter-cultural. It is also to do as Jesus did, and be as Jesus was.

Two modern monastics write of humility in ways that illuminate its occurrence in Mary of Egypt's story, in which humility

---

94. Ward, *Desert Christian,* 247.

95. Walsh, "Ascetic Mother," 60.

96. For a very helpful contemporary treatment see Andre Louf, *The Way of Humility*, trans. Lawrence S. Cunningham, MW 11 (Kalamazoo, MI: Cistercian Publications, 2007).

is "bestowed on the most unlikely of characters,"[97] a harlot and a prideful monk. In a chapter in *New Seeds of Contemplation* entitled "Humility against Despair," Thomas Merton, OCSO, suggests, "perfect humility implies perfect confidence in the power of God, before Whom no other power has any meaning."[98] Mary of Egypt faced perfect humility when she encountered the icon of the Virgin Mary and continued to have perfect confidence in God's power experienced through the Blessed Mother. "Humility," writes Michael Casey, OCSO, "is not primarily a social virtue. . . . It is the necessary consequence that follows an encounter with the loving holiness of God. After that it doesn't matter much what status others assign to us."[99] Zossima's "encounter with the loving holiness of God" occurred when he encountered Mary of Egypt, in whom he experienced perfect humility, which led him to more complete human-ness.

As is well known, *human* and *humble* are rooted in the Latin words *humilis*, low (as in "not high," not God, for example) and *humus*, "earth." We are *hum*an beings, all made of the "dust of the ground" (i.e., dirt), and therefore all share the same low status. Rightly to understand our humanity is to understand that, fundamentally, none of us is superior to, but, importantly, each is the same as others. It might be easy to feel superior to Mary. Zossima might well have done so. But as David Keller eloquently explains, "her hedonistic behavior never destroyed the image of God within her."[100] Her sexual desire did not quench a latent desire for God. The former (sexual desire) was a distorted version of the latter (desire for God).

Symbolically, Mary's sexual hunger was the outward, visible manifestation of a spiritual hunger that was much more profound.

97. Posa, "Mary and Zossima," 8.

98. Thomas Merton, *New Seeds of Contemplation* (New York: New Directions, 1961), 190.

99. Michael Casey, *Balaam's Donkey* (Collegeville, MN: Liturgical Press, 2019), 216.

100. Keller, *Oasis of Wisdom,* 150–51.

The final stanza of a poem by Irish patriot, Padraic H. Pearse, beautifully expresses the idea:

> O woman that no lover's kiss
> (Tho' many a kiss was given thee)
> Could slake thy love, is it not for this
> The hero Christ shall die for thee?[101]

As did Christ, Mary empties herself (Phil 2:7). Seeking the help of the Blessed Virgin is a form of withdrawal from self-assertion, a turning from the past and opening to transformation, as Keller writes: "the power of self-emptying becomes the womb of *collaborating with God.*"[102]

Eventually, Mary's collaboration also heals and humanizes Zossima. He had been a monk from infancy and apparently thought that no one could teach him anything. His lust was for perfection, so he had gone to the famous Jordan River monasteries. In the one he entered, it was the practice to go into the desert for Lent; there he meets Mary of Egypt. As in the meeting of Abba Anthony and Abba Paul of Thebes, each begs blessing from the other, and Zossima recognizes that grace is "not by office but by gifts of the spirit."[103] He humbles himself by asking *her* for help, and thereby both repents of his arrogance and receives his humanity. God's presence in Mary was the oasis of wisdom for Zossima.[104]

The mutual submission and deepening humanity of both Mary and Zossima are the fruit of their humility, a humility that both arises and develops from self-knowledge. Humility, notes *The Oxford Dictionary of the Christian Church,* is "an aspect of truth-

---

101. A version of this poem is sung by the monks of Glenstal Abbey at Vespers on the Feast of Saint Mary Magdalene. I quote from the liner notes of *Vox de Nube*, Nóirín Ní Riain and Monks of Glenstal, Dublin: Gael-Linn, 1989, compact disc. Pearse wrote in Gaelic and died in the April 1916 uprising.

102. Keller, *Oasis of Wisdom,* 151. Bold type in the original.

103. Keller, *Oasis of Wisdom,* 152.

104. Keller, *Oasis of Wisdom,* 153.

fulness, neither exaggerating nor denigrating the truth of what one is."[105] Thomas Merton (perhaps via Thomas Aquinas) writes, "perfect humility and perfect integrity coincide." And again, "humility consists in being precisely the person you actually are before God."[106] Before the icon of the Virgin Mary, Mary of Egypt recognizes who she is: the harlot and God's beloved. Her accurate self-knowledge fires her resulting action. Zossima's high evaluation of himself is shattered when he realizes his shortcomings in relation to Mary of the desert, and this realization leads him to repentance and growth. In both cases, humility is manifested in accurate self-knowledge and change in light of it (William James's criteria for true conversion).

Clearly the theological interests of the Mary of Egypt narrative are sunk deep in the theological soil of monasticism, its *conversatio morum*, virtues, and attitudes. But these fundamental aspects of monasticism that flourish in Mary's story are easily transplanted into the stony or thorny or good soil of the lives of the laity. As God dealt mercifully with Mary and Zossima, so God might deal with anyone. And for lay listeners (as for monks), the encounter was likely to come in the context of religious observances and practices. They too appear and have an educative function in Mary's story. As the subtitle of Ward's chapter on Mary of Egypt reminds us, monastic theology and spiritual practices are not disconnected in her story.[107]

Sacraments, Icons, and Relics

The versions of Mary of Egypt's story reflect not only theology, but Christian spiritual practices of the times when they were composed. The most well-known and practiced were the biblical sacraments of baptism and Eucharist, the veneration of icons, and

---

105. Cross and Livingstone, *Oxford Dictionary,* 804, col. 2.
106. Merton, *New Seeds of Contemplation,* 99.
107. Ward, *Harlots of the Desert,* 26–56, chap. 3.

devotion to relics. A case can be made that the veneration of icons itself accounts for Mary's conversion and the literature that arose from it. Indeed, as was noted in the introduction, the "conversion of Mary of Egypt is cited by John of Damascus (d. ca. 750) in his *De imaginibus* as an instance of the efficacy of icons."[108] Similarly, the two biblical sacraments of baptism and Eucharist appear at critical points in the narrative. They are outward and visible signs of the inward and spiritual events in the characters' lives. The references to baptism signal new beginnings, and the narrative itself moves toward the *dénouement* of Mary's reception of the Eucharist at the hands of Zossima. Mary's life of sanctity begins and ends with Christian sacraments.

In Canto 6 of the verse life of Mary by Hildebert of Lavardin (d. 1134), Mary stresses that her parents, "Often imparted to me in my tender age the precepts of a strict life."[109] In his rendering of Mary of Egypt's life, which follows French manuscripts, an anonymous Spanish poet of the thirteenth century writes, "She was baptized as an infant, / Then she was educated."[110] The translators note that "Sometimes he [the poet] is inaccurate and sometimes he is creative. He adds little touches of humanity and realism to the story he is translating."[111] Medieval Christian readers and hearers would, of course, have expected that good parents had had their infants baptized, so perhaps Mary was, or perhaps the detail was added.

The "second" baptism of Mary is volitional and occurs after her encounter with the icon of the Blessed Virgin. Mary of Egypt goes to "the Church of John the Baptist near the Jordan, and having prayed in the church, I went down immediately to the Jordan

108. John of Damascus, *De imaginibus*, PG 94:1415–18, quoted in Magennis, "Conversion," 307 n. 43.

109. In Pepin and Feiss, *Saint Mary of Egypt*, 89.

110. Pepin and Feiss, *Saint Mary of Egypt*, 119.

111. Pepin and Feiss, *Saint Mary of Egypt*, 41–42.

and washed my hands and face in its holy water."[112] The monks and lay people for whom Mary's story was preserved would, of course, recognize John the Baptist, whose preaching associated baptism with "the remission of sins." Mark 1:4-5 records that "all the people of Jerusalem were going out to him, and were baptized by him in the river Jordan, confessing their sins." This is, more or less, what Mary of Egypt did, although (and we will return to this point) Mary baptizes herself. Because she had already been baptized? Because, at this stage in her spiritual journey, she could not entrust herself to *any* man, even a priest? Because in most of the narrative she is outside the "walls" of the institutional church?

Although Christian theology asserts that there is "one Lord, one faith, one baptism" (Eph 4:5), some branches of the Christian family have practiced "re-baptism" for various reasons. Certainly one could read (as several scholars have) the text as Mary's *symbolic* cleansing of herself to mark the end of her sinful life. Similarly, the voice she heard at the church said, "If you cross over the Jordan, you will find rest."[113] "Crossing the Jordan" is a common Judeo-Christian metaphor for "beginning anew." To "cross the Jordan" is to enter the Promised Land, the land God gives the chosen, whether that is Canaan or heaven.

In several tellings of Mary's story, Zossima too crosses the Jordan. The monastery's Lenten practice was to cross the Jordan into the desert: "So Zosimas, following the customary rule of the monastery, crossed the Jordan."[114] In some tellings, on his first crossing he used a small boat, perhaps a symbol of the church? If so, the church was the vehicle of his conversion in taking him to Mary of Egypt. It keeps him safely in the *ekklesia*. Several accounts of this event suggest that the medieval poets understood the symbol of crossing the Jordan, which became for Zossima, too, an entrance into enlightened self-knowledge and deeper spiritual

112. Ward, *Harlots of the Desert,* 49.
113. Ward, *Harlots of the Desert,* 48.
114. Kouli, "Life of St. Mary of Egypt," 74–75.

understanding. On his second meeting with Mary, "he saw her signing the waters of the Jordan with the sign of the Cross." Then "she stepped on to the water and walking over the flowing waves she came as if walking on solid land."[115] Rather than an image of baptism, this Jordan crossing is intended to allude to Jesus' walking on the water (Mark 6:45-51; Matt 14:22-27; John 6:16-21). Would the implied Christ-Mary connection also have been a reference to shared or perfected humility?

The second biblical sacrament, the Eucharist, also marks the beginning and end of Mary's conscious spiritual journey. After she has washed herself in the Jordan near the Church of St. John the Baptist, she says, "Then I made my communion of the most pure and life-giving Sacrament of Christ the Lord, in the Church of St. John, Forerunner and Baptist."[116] She takes the initiative to seek the sacrament (an act suggesting that she *was* baptized and properly instructed as a child). She would not receive it again for some forty-seven or forty-eight years, when she once more takes the initiative to ask Fr. Zossima to bring her "a portion of the life-giving Body and Blood in a holy vessel . . . and bring it to me on the bank of the Jordan . . . so that . . . I may receive the life-giving gifts."[117] Walsh says, "In doing this, Mary is identifying herself as a disciple of Christ within the context of the Church."[118] Zossima did as she asked. A year later he brings her the Eucharist, and "she received the life-giving gifts of the sacrament, groaning and weeping,"[119] prayed the *Nunc Dimittis* ("Lord, now let thy servant depart in peace," Luke 2:29-32), and died shortly thereafter.

115. Ward, *Harlots of the Desert*, 53.

116. Ward, *Harlots of the Desert*, 49.

117. Ward, *Harlots of the Desert*, 51. That Mary calls the Eucharist the "Body and Blood" reflects the authoritative pronouncement of the Fourth Lateran Council (1215) on transubstantiation and reflects another catechetical contribution of Mary's story to its hearers, one perhaps added by a medieval teller of her story.

118. Walsh, "Ascetic Mother," 66.

119. Ward, *Harlots of the Desert*, 53.

Mary's spiritual journey begins and ends with the sacraments. She was probably baptized as an infant and re-baptizes herself in the Jordan, symbolizing her new beginning. It is only *after* her full confession to Fr. Zossima, her autobiography, which is the heart of the story in the traditional narratives, that she receives absolution from him, and later the Eucharist. The proper ecclesial requirements are fulfilled in her story, and, again, Walsh suggests "Sanctification, deification occurs within the sacramental Church,"[120] though outside their conventional settings.

The communication of ideas, and thus of theology, has never been a matter of language alone. And literacy has only recently become widespread in human history. Before the book, there was oral transmission of story and idea; there was music and song,[121] and what could be touched and seen. Artistic, symbolic representation of Christian ideas and persons makes important contributions to church history and theology. Across the Christian world ancient fresco, mosaic, and carved ivory suggest that the Christian story was from its inception communicated visually. One thinks of the *ichthus* or "fish" symbol, the ship that symbolized the church, catacomb paintings. Nicolas Zernov explains, "The colours and designs of the ikons, the sound of the sacred songs, the domes and arches of the buildings dedicated to the celebration of the divine mystery . . . form an integral and indispensable part of worship."[122]

Icons are not simply pictures with religious content. As Zernov says, they "are prayers enshrined in painted wood." To see icons, Zernov explains, is "to gaze through these windows into the world beyond time and space." He continues, icons "differ from religious

120. Walsh, "Ascetic Mother," 66.

121. Quotation of hymns in the Pauline letters suggests Christology was first sung. See Luke Timothy Johnson, *Religious Experience in Earliest Christianity* (Minneapolis: Fortress Press, 1998); Robert J. Karris, *A Symphony of New Testament Hymns* (Collegeville, MN: Liturgical Press, 1996); Daniel Liderback, *Christ in the Early Christian Hymns* (New York: Paulist Press, 1998).

122. Nicolas Zernov, *Eastern Christendom* (London: Weidenfeld and Nicolson, 1961), 276.

paintings by the symbolic treatment of their subjects, by their special technique of design and colouring, and above all by the change in their substance through the love and transforming prayer of those who made them and those who venerate them."[123] Icons of saints, and biblical and liturgical events, and symbolic presentations of theological ideas painted on wood in egg tempera, were numerous in the East by the fifth century. Two iconoclastic controversies roiled the church for several hundred years and were unfortunate steps toward the Great Schism, but the icons themselves continued to be an important part of public and private devotion in the Eastern churches and have in recent years made a comeback in the popular devotion of the Western church.

Mary of Egypt was apparently converted by her encounter with an icon of the Blessed Virgin Mary. By this time, Walsh says, "icons of Christ and of the Theotokos begin to have symbolic power. . . . Holy men had introduced and supported the use of icons in Church. Icons and saints are intimately related. In both, one sees the divine plan in operation."[124] According to Zernov, "The saints whom they represented . . . looked straight into the eyes of their beholders and desired to remain operative in the lives of their fellow Christians."[125] This certainly seems to have been the case in Mary of Egypt's experience with the Blessed Virgin Mary's icon.

Not surprisingly, Mary of Egypt has been widely portrayed in icons. As noted earlier, Mary of Magdalene and Mary of Egypt have often been confused and conflated in Western hagiographical art. But as Heron observes, "Orthodox iconography more faithfully portrays Mary in her hoary, elderly, and androgonous [*sic*] state."[126] Kouli concurs that "In Byzantine art the saint is

123. Zernov, *Eastern Christendom,* 277. A very helpful and beautifully illustrated study of icons is Leonid Ouspensky and Vladimir Lossky, *The Meaning of Icons* (Crestwood, NY: St. Vladimir's Seminary Press, 1989).

124. Walsh, "Ascetic Mother," 64.

125. Zernov, *Eastern Christendom,* 277.

126. Heron, "Lioness," 41.

depicted as an androgynous figure, extremely thin with a dark complexion. Her emaciated body is partly covered by a piece of cloth, representing the cloak offered her by Zosimas during their first encounter."[127] Icons of Mary of Egypt appear to follow one of three basic patterns. In the first Mary is depicted alone as a thin, old woman draped in a cloth, or occasionally covered by her long, white hair. In many of these, one of her hands gestures toward the other that holds up a cross, or she reaches out to a depiction of the Blessed Virgin in an upper corner. In another she stands holding the three small loaves she took into the desert, and behind her, across the Jordan, is the lion. This template also sometimes has Mary standing alone *on* the Jordan River.

In a second pattern, white-haired Mary stands in the desert with the Jordan behind her, draped in a cloth with her hands crossed demurely on her chest on which her ribs are visible. Grouped around her, sometimes in small medallions, are important events in her *vita*, for example, meeting Zossima, Zossima turned away offering her a cloak, Mary walking across the Jordan, and her corpse being buried by Zossima and the lion. Again, the Blessed Virgin Mary sometimes appears in an upper corner looking benevolently down.

In the third pattern, Zossima and Mary stand beside the Jordan River. She is an emaciated, white-haired woman, reaching a hand toward the priest who is holding a covered chalice and offering Mary Communion in a spoon. In some versions, she holds one side, he the other of the cloth that prevents the consecrated elements from falling to the ground, recognizably the Orthodox form of receiving the Eucharist. These patterns (and there may

---

127. Kouli, "Life of St. Mary of Egypt," 68. A detailed discussion of Mary's iconography in Byzantine art has been written by N. K. Moutsopoulos and G. Demetrokalles and published in Thessalonike in 1981, but to my knowledge it is available only in Greek. A collection of depictions of Mary in Western art has been prepared by Manuel Alvar, ed., *Vida de Santa Maria Egipciaca*, vol. 2 (Madrid: Clasicos Hispanicos, 1970).

be others) are not rigid. Aspects of one may appear in another. A great deal could be (and has been) written about the symbols in these icons. In most Mary's hands are reaching out in supplication or to receive.

In some writings of the icon Mary is depicted as dark-skinned, and she is so described in some of the texts. The viewer's first conclusion is that her skin has been bronzed and burnt by desert dwelling. But in the texts, by her own admission, she comes from the Nile in "Egypt," which in the fifth century AD did not have the current national boundaries. Alexandria, of course, was on the Mediterranean. But the Nile flows in sub-Saharan Africa. From how far south of Alexandria on the Nile did Mary come? Icons depict their subjects both symbolically and with great accuracy.

When queried about the depiction of Mary's ethnology, iconographer Sr. Kay Kettenhofen, OCSO, noted that

> The color of her skin tone is interesting. When Zosima first catches a glimpse of her he is afraid it is the devil. That would be a natural assumption if he saw a black body. Depending on the tradition icon painters are working in, the basic underpainting for the skin is usually either greenish or brownish which would look like an intended dark rendering of the skin and not be an indication that the person was of negro origin.[128]

Both the literary and the iconic evidence are inconclusive. But it would be interesting to know whether the earliest icons of Mary of Egypt depicted her with darker skin. More recent ones do not. Could a great saint of Caucasian Europe have been an African woman? Has she, as her contemporary Saint Augustine of Hippo perhaps has, been "bleached" by European history?[129]

128. From an email to me from Sr. Kay on August 5, 2020.
129. There is lively debate about the ethnic heritage of Saint Augustine. He was born in Thagaste, Numidia, now Algeria. Some scholars say he is descended from Punic (ancient Phoenician) settlers in Africa; others say that his mother was a Berber. Icons depict him with a wide range of skin tones. The *National*

What I find when looking into the face of the white-haired, wrinkled, emaciated old body depicted in the icons is a beautiful woman. It is no small feat that even the least competent writings manage to evoke a woman of great sorrow and great beauty, which are of course the two poles of her story.[130] As Zernov explains, the figural patterns and symbols in icons invite the on-looker to enter the story, "to gaze through these windows into the world beyond time and space."[131] To paraphrase what Thomas Hill writes of emblematic narratives, in icons inner experience is reflected by the external events depicted. Visible reality not only "represents invisible reality,"[132] but invites us to enter it. And sometimes this looking or gazing reveals to the on-looker unexpected things.

It seems to be a universal human impulse to want spiritual realities to "put skin (whatever its color) on," to be in some way visible or tangible. This impulse reflects something of the mysterious genius of Christ's incarnation. "God is spirit," says Jesus to the Samaritan woman (John 4:24), and we are to worship "in spirit and in truth" (John 4:23). But something tangible and physical helps: a bit of bread, a sip of wine, an icon, a carpenter from Galilee to make visible and corporeal the Spirit-God. Christian icons spoke and speak to this perceived need. So do relics, physical remains of spiritual paradigms, or objects they came in contact with, things like the healing handkerchiefs that had touched Saint Paul's body (Acts 19:12). The cult of relics spread quickly in the early church. The Second Nicaean Council (787 A.D.) decreed that no church could be consecrated without one. That there were abuses connected with relics is undeniable, but equally undeniable are the accounts of those who have venerated them and been helped and healed.

Catholic Reporter for November 13, 2013, included him in a series featuring Black saints. James J. O'Donnell of Georgetown University has written an online discussion of Saint Augustine that addresses the matter.

130. As in most icons, it is, I think, something about the character of the eyes, which I always find returning my gaze.

131. Zernov, *Eastern Christendom,* 277.

132. Hill, *"Imago Dei,"* 45.

Not surprisingly, there is widespread evidence of relics of Mary of Egypt, even though the location of her burial and body was unknown. The relics were considered especially potent since she, and thus they, had direct connection with the true cross, Christ's tomb, and a vision of His Mother. According to one account quoted by Walsh, "In 1059 Luke, Abbot of Carbonne in Calabria, carried her entire body from Jerusalem and placed the body in the Abbey Church." However, as Walsh notes, "there are relics of Mary's body in Rome and all over Spain, Italy, Portugal, and elsewhere."[133] In a fifteenth-century reference to relics in Westminster Abbey, London, mention is made of parts of Mary's skull from the collection of Queen Emma (d. 1052).[134]

Whatever else evidence of Mary's relics is or isn't, it certainly proves Mary of Egypt's wide-spread popularity for nearly a thousand years of Christian history. But ancient tales of talking icons, water-walking reformed harlots, elderly monks, and undertaker lions? What can they possibly have to say to us?

Contemporary Interest

Contemporary interest in Mary of Egypt does not imply that the traditional theological concerns of her story are no longer relevant. The psychological and spiritual aspects of conversion and penitence continue to be of importance to Christians. Mariology and the implications of its history have garnered great theological interest in contemporary scholarship, and the discussion of humility is, and will be, a source of on-going debate. Several of the important theological concerns and Christian practices in the narrative of Mary of Egypt made it of catechetical value in both the monastic and the secular worlds of earlier Christian eras. Another aspect of the story, which may especially resonate with contemporary readers, has generated a number of recent scholarly studies. What has

133. Walsh, "Ascetic Mother," 68.
134. Magennis, *Old English Life,* 12.

drawn scholars' attention is a source of perennial fascination: the relationship of men and women, gender roles, and, tangentially, the roles of women in and women's relationship to the institutional church. After some observations about Mary and about Zossima I will highlight some "contemporary" features of their relationship.

Although the poems with which this book opens do not preserve the original narrative's structure of a tale within a tale (that is, they do not begin and end with Zossima's story as a frame for Mary's telling of hers), I hope the new verse life preserves what Simon Lavery calls a complex double structure in which each story is a foil to the other. Every feature of Mary's story, he notes, is significant in its own right and fulfills a function in Zossima's quest.[135] In effect, this means that one must read the two stories together properly to understand their import. The parallelism is the key to the gender lesson in the text.

The depiction of Mary of Egypt in the historical narrative reveals a woman of autonomy, immorality, and eventually holiness. Jane Stevenson interprets it as misogynistic, suggesting that "Mary's characterization of her youthful self is very much a creation of male paranoia about women."[136] At an early age she left the social structure of family and village and set out to make her own way in the world. This eventually turns out to be, says Magennis, a "holy subversion of social expectations,"[137] even though the narrative evokes traditional attitudes toward prostitutes, and even though, since Mary doesn't take money for sex, she isn't technically a prostitute.[138] She travels alone, eventually into the desert, the place of danger and, for her, repentant holiness. The hinge of her story is the events in Jerusalem at the Church of the Holy Sepulcher/Resurrection.

135. Lavery, "Story of Mary," 128.
136. Stevenson, "Holy Sinner," 26.
137. Magennis, "St. Mary of Egypt and Aelfric," 107.
138. For an extended discussion of attitudes toward prostitutes in medieval England, see Lavery, "Story of Mary," 138–42.

Of particular interest to contemporary scholars has been that Mary's conversion is outside the structures of the male hierarchy of the institutional church. She goes to Jerusalem under her own steam (although some of her companions are on pilgrimage), decides on her own (out of curiosity?) to see a relic of the Holy Cross, and when unable to enter the church, encounters the Blessed Virgin Mary to whom she says, "Receive my confession."[139] It is the Virgin Mary who grants the Egyptian entrance to the church, she who directs Mary to the desert. Walsh suggests "that the Theotokos was the one who freed Mary, suggests a possible female-saved-by-female motif."[140] It is Mary of Egypt who re-baptizes herself in the Jordan near the church of the Baptizer and, having received the Eucharist, crosses into the desert where she remains under the protection of the Virgin to whom she prays.

In the minds of the pious, Mary's independent life in the desert must have evoked those of Elijah, of John the Baptist, and of Jesus. She exemplifies an Eastern model of what Coon calls "extra-institutional power of living anchorites."[141] In the medieval world, especially in England, there was a tradition of anchorites who (perhaps after a liturgical service of enclosure, but perhaps not) lived exemplary lives of great asceticism and holiness. For example, the thirteenth-century *Ancrene Wisse* was written to guide anchoresses.[142] An anchoress who is currently widely known was Julian of Norwich, who died sometime after 1416. At the time of Dame Julian, and earlier, as Magennis writes, "The *Life of St. Mary of Egypt* would have been seen by an informed Anglo-Saxon reader as presenting a "radically alternative spiritual ideal."[143] Recent feminist interpretations read in these very ancient narra-

139. Ward, *Harlots of the Desert,* 47.

140. Walsh, "Ascetic Mother," 67.

141. Coon, *Sacred Fictions,* 85.

142. See Anne Savage and Nicholas Watson, trans., *Anchoritic Spirituality: Ancrene Wisse and Associated Works* (New York: Paulist Press, 1991).

143. Magennis, *Old English Life,* 24.

tives a woman who flouted convention, lived autonomously, and was sanctified beyond the confines of the patriarchal institution of the church.

What of Zossima? He represents the male hierarchy and is the moral mirror opposite of Mary of Egypt. Given to the monastery as a child (a recognized and not infrequent familial practice in medieval Europe as well), he was in every way an exemplary monk. No one, so he thought, exceeded him in monastic doctrine or practice. So his spiritual quest led him to seek more austere and perfect monasteries. In some manuscripts of this narrative, an ancient monk directs him to the Judean desert where, since the monks don't speak of their Lenten desert experiences, there can be no opportunity for competition in asceticism. Lavery suggests that the remarkable life of Mary is balanced by the blameless one, the "dull narrative of Zossima's progressive austerity,"[144] in order to preclude either lascivious or pious readers from misinterpreting the meaning of the narrative. Mary's lusts are bodily, and she conquers them in the desert. Zossima's lust is for perfection manifested in his pride. Fr. Zossima, write Srs. Katherine and Thekla, "was on the road of lovelessness and death."[145] But Zossima's lust, too, is conquered in the desert by the example of the ex-harlot Mary of Egypt. Pride meets humility. Humility wins.

After explaining Mary's lack of legal status in late antiquity— noting that women like her were called "human vermin" in some documents—Stevenson observes that Zossima "is humble and acute enough to see that a discarded scrap of human garbage might be both a great lady, and a vehicle for great truths." That, Stevenson says, would have been a jolt to original audiences.[146] For medieval monastic audiences, Lavery points out that Zossima's recognition of Mary's spiritual superiority "is the climax of the process of self-discovery which is the focus of interest in

---

144. Lavery, "Story of Mary," 124.
145. Sr. Katherine and Sr. Thekla, *St. Andrew of Crete,* 24.
146. Stevenson, "Holy Sinner," 28.

this text."[147] In perhaps a return to its original message, by the medieval period the story's focus has shifted from penitent harlot repents and is saved, to spiritual pride.

On the face of it one might read this tale as a sixth-century feminist manifesto in which a woman dominates both narratively and spiritually. While I laud Mary of Egypt, this reading is facile if it divorces the tale from its origins in Christian theology and monastic spirituality. And I am always wary of reading back onto earlier eras, ideas or theories that did not then exist. I agree that the tale exhibits "extraordinary gender dynamics" but resist what Heron refers to as the "recognition of Zossima's emasculated status on the one hand, and Mary's role as immasculated woman on the other."[148] This work is, indeed, as Scheil writes, a "narrative of extremes and oppositions,"[149] but the oppositions suggest what is in the final analysis an image of healthy reciprocity.

Lavery has highlighted the "network of contrasts" (or "parallels") between Mary and Zossima: priest/proud; courtesan/penitent; abstinent/spiritually indulgent. Each story begins in one place (city, locus of sin/monastery, locus of holiness), and the two converge in the desert (locus of transformation). Mary is outwardly ugly and solitary but inwardly beautiful and perfect. The fun of the story, Lavery suggests, is the resolution of opposites.[150] In support of this reading, I suggest that each character provides something the other lacks. For all her autonomy and outside-the-camp life, in the narrative Mary realizes she needs Father Zossima's blessing and the Holy Eucharist, which he, as a priest of the church, can provide. For all his self-satisfaction and monastic perfection, Zossima realizes in Mary a humility and humanity that he lacks. Some of the variant versions subtly hint that he comes to love Mary in a way that completes his humanity. (One remembers

147. Lavery, "Story of Mary," 127.
148. Heron, "Lioness," 25.
149. Scheil, "Bodies and Boundaries," 137.
150. Lavery, "Story of Mary," 129–30.

here the late-life passion of Thomas Merton, OCSO, for a young nurse, and its maturing effect on that twentieth-century priest/monk.) Lavery suggests that the tale is "a spiritual love story in Zossima's yearning for Mary."[151] Zossima is edified by a woman outside the pale, and Mary is fed by a priest very much inside the structure or institution. At many levels the opposites in the narrative are reconciled.

The earliest texts of the story do indeed show what Stevenson calls the "harmonious integration of opposing forces" in sixth-century Christianity.[152] And as Lavery says, the two quests "end in mutual fulfillment."[153] Seen in one light, the story closes with an image of "Eden restored." The separation (if not hostility) between the sexes is resolved by a healthy reciprocity of opposites and an image of complementarity. And if the lion doesn't lie down with the human, at least it doesn't eat him, but helps him dig a grave, providing the image of a peaceable kingdom in which human and animal cooperate.

Conclusion

Finally, someone might ask: Why spend half a lifetime thinking about a saint who might not have existed? The most honest answer is because I am intrigued by the person and character (in all three senses) of Mary of Egypt, the literary brilliance of her *vita*, and the fascinating history and moral of her story.[154] The literary history and devices of the story are compelling, and the number of scholarly essays over many years and in several languages suggest that many scholars have found it so. When Dolger explains "the place of Byzantine literature in the general context of medieval literature," he says that "it was a formative influence in the

---

151. Lavery, "Story of Mary," 122.
152. Stevenson, "Holy Sinner," 23.
153. Lavery, "Story of Mary," 129.
154. And, I feel oddly chosen for this task, called to it.

spirituality of the middle ages."[155] He writes that the Greek Fathers of the fourth and fifth centuries "produced works which from the literary and philosophical point of view could hold their own with their pagan opponents; thus in their writings they transformed the tidings of redemption . . . and ensured their survival."[156] He continues, "Byzantium added much to the rich store of medieval European folk tales, for it was the great clearing house of East and West."[157] Additionally, Mary of Egypt's story raises at least three subjects that are of perennial interest: relationships between genders (which in our day includes the relationship of women to the institutional church), sin and forgiving grace, and the problem of human judgments.

First, Zossima is the vehicle for Mary's story. Granted, had he not told it after her death, we wouldn't know it. But the real "juice and joy" (to borrow three words from Gerard Manley Hopkins) of the tale is Mary's story.[158] There are many "sinner to saint" stories, but Mary's is particularly appealing, in part because it is a woman's story, and a woman (THE woman, Jesus' mother) facilitates her conversion. Then Mary of Egypt, in turn, facilitates a priest's spiritual journey. But it reads an old story through too modern a lens to conclude that this is a story of a woman saved outside the male, institutional church. Mary went to the Mother Church in Jerusalem, and there, by the grace of Christ's mother, was able to venerate the relics of his cross. She, the consummate sinner, proceeded to the Jordan, to the Church of John the Baptist (he who preached repentance to sinners), and received the Eucharist. She asked Zossima to bring her Holy Communion. Mary's spiritual autonomy is balanced by what the male, institutional church offers her.

155. Dolger, "Byzantine Literature," 262.

156. Dolger, "Byzantine Literature," 262.

157. Dolger, "Byzantine Literature," 263.

158. "Spring," in *The Poems of Gerard Manley Hopkins,* ed. W. H. Gardner and N. H. MacKenzie, 4th ed. (Oxford: Oxford University Press, 1972), 69.

Similarly, Fr. Zossima's sin is of another category, but certainly a terrible one for a Christian and a monk. He desperately needs what he finds in Mary of Egypt. Her abject humility confounds his pride. As Norris writes, "The monk who encounters Mary still has a lot to learn; his understanding of the spiritual life is facile in comparison to hers, and he knows it."[159] As noted earlier, Srs. Katherine and Thekla observe that "Father Zossima was on the road of lovelessness and death. . . . Father Zossima was roused to the clarity of vision which can only come *from* love and be directed *to* Love."[160]

Posa's excellent article on Mary and Zossima is sub-titled "Icons of Mutuality in the Spiritual Journey."[161] Mary's is a story of reciprocity. Paradigmatically, when she first meets Zossima, each asks blessing of the other. Each of the two main characters needs what the other can offer. The woman and the man need each other. The self-appointed anchoress "outside the camp" needs what only the church that Zossima represents can give. Posa's summary is exactly correct: "the possibility of transformation in Christ, of both the feminine and masculine domains takes place in a radical openness to each other—in a stance that is profoundly open to listening to the story of the other and honestly telling one's own."[162] And, as she notes, "it is only in the telling of this story within a relationship of mutuality that transformation is ultimately effected."[163]

Posa's observations lead to the second recurring interest of the story: sin and forgiving grace. Both main characters demonstrate the truth of Posa's dictum: "In the burdens that we carry around with us, the burden of our own history is the heaviest."[164] The

---

159. Norris, *Cloister Walk,* 166.

160. Sr. Katherine and Sr. Thekla, *St. Andrew of Crete*, 24. Italics in original.

161. Posa, "Mary and Zossima," 5.

162. Posa, "Mary and Zossima," 21.

163. Posa, "Mary and Zossima," 20.

164. Posa, "Mary and Zossima," 20.

story of Mary's sin is told in luscious detail and with great energy. Zossima's failings may be less overtly dramatic, but are no less sin. Both in their own ways find forgiving grace. Regardless of the historical epoch, the Mary of Egypt narrative is a story for penitent sinners, all of whom are objects of God's love and forgiveness. As did Mary, some have great, public infidelities to mourn. Others, like Zossima, have secret sins of pride and self-congratulation. All have sins of commission and of omission, what we have done, left undone, and ought not to have done, to paraphrase the *Book of Common Prayer*. Even if, like Zossima, we think ourselves flawless, we are sinners because we are enmeshed in unjust political and economic systems, communal greed, and blindness to the sufferings of others. But Mary and Zossima's is a story, to borrow from Julia H. Johnson's hymn, of "Grace that exceeds our sin and our guilt."[165] If God could forgive a profligate like Mary of Egypt, as the narrative shows that God did, if God could forgive a self-righteous old stick like Zossima, as the narrative shows that God did, then God could forgive *anyone*. The "old, old story/Of Jesus and His love"[166] is always new and often news.

Third and finally, when it comes to the matter of who is a sinner and who is to judge, the story of Mary of Egypt suggests that things may not be as they appear on the surface. A remarkable portion of the teaching of Jesus in the New Testament warns his hearers about judging because they "judge by human standards" (John 8:15), that is, by appearances or by what is temporal. A harlot may be a saint. An apparently flawless monk and priest may be on very thin spiritual ice. This is part of the perpetual pleasure of this narrative: the apparent "bad one" turns out not to be, and the "good one" learns a few things from her.

Human beings don't know the whole story. Only God can see people's hearts and motivations. Srs. Katherine and Thekla write, "we do not know, nor are we meant to know, into the Mind of

---

165. Julia H. Johnston, 1849–1919, "Grace Greater than Our Sin."
166. A. Catherine Hankey, 1834–1911, "I Love to Tell the Story."

God and, hence, we can not judge His values."[167] Jesus said, "Do not judge, and you will not be judged" (Luke 6:37; Matt 7:1). "Forgive, and you will be forgiven" (Luke 6:37). And the biblical punch line in the book of James is "mercy triumphs over judgment" (Jas 2:13). James's statement summarizes the plot of the Mary of Egypt narrative. "How should we be able to deny that he [Zossima] was good and that she [Mary of Egypt] was bad?" ask Srs. Katherine and Thekla. "Yet, the whole crux of the story hangs on this one point of seeming-vice and seeming-virtue and the mercy of God who allowed the two parallel lines to meet before it was too late." "We do not know the value of any thought or any action," they write. "And so we repent."[168] And so, the story shows, we are forgiven.

"From now on, therefore," Saint Paul wrote to the church at Corinth, "we regard no one from a human point of view. . . . If anyone is in Christ, there is a new creation: everything old has passed away; see, everything has become new! All this is from God, who reconciled us to himself through Christ" (2 Cor 5:16-18). The *vita* of Saint Mary of Egypt is an example of the truth of Paul's text, and in every age it is good news.

167. Sr. Katherine and Sr. Thekla, *St. Andrew of Crete,* 24.
168. Sr. Katherine and Sr. Thekla, *St. Andrew of Crete,* 24.

Select Bibliography

Because Saint Mary of Egypt was so popular in late antiquity and the medieval period, there is a vast secondary literature on her story in several European languages, especially in French, German, Greek, and Spanish. I have confined the following suggestions for further reading to English studies, largely those used in the preparation of this book.

Lives of Saint Mary of Egypt in English Translation

Srs. Katherine and Thekla, trans. and eds. *St. Andrew of Crete (The Great Canon) St. Mary of Egypt (The Life)*. Library of Orthodox Thinking. Filgrave, Buckinghamshire, and Normanby, N. Yorkshire, UK: Greek Orthodox Monastery, 1974.

Kouli, Maria, trans. "Life of St. Mary of Egypt." In *Holy Women of Byzantium: Ten Saints' Lives in English Translation,* edited by Alice-Mary Talbot. Washington, DC: Dumbarton Oaks Research Library and Collection, 1996. 65–93.

Magennis, Hugh, trans. *The Old English Life of St. Mary of Egypt*. Exeter: University of Exeter Press, 2002.

Pepin, Ronald, and Hugh Feiss, trans. *Saint Mary of Egypt: Three Medieval Lives in Verse*. CS 209. Kalamazoo, MI: Cistercian Publications, 2005.

Talbot, Alice-Mary, ed. *Holy Women of Byzantium: Ten Saints' Lives in English Translation*. Washington, DC: Dumbarton Oaks Research Library and Collection, 1996.

Ward, Benedicta. *Harlots of the Desert: A Study of Repentance in Early Monastic Sources*. CS 106. Kalamazoo, MI: Cistercian Publications, 1987.

Ward, Benedicta. English translation of *The Life of Our Holy Mother Mary of Egypt* by Sophronius, from the Latin of Paul the Deacon. http://ocf.org/OrthodoxPage/reading/st.mary.html.

Studies of Saint Mary of Egypt

Carter, E. D. "Mary of Egypt, St." *New Catholic Encyclopedia*. Washington, DC: Catholic University Press, 1967.

Chaudhari, Pia Sophia. "Depth Psychology and the Courage of St. Mary of Egypt." *Public Orthodoxy*. The Orthodox Christian Studies Center, Fordham University. https://publicorthodoxy.org. Accessed April 1, 2020.

Coon, Lynda L. *Sacred Fictions: Holy Women and Hagiography in Late Antiquity*. Philadelphia: University of Pennsylvania Press, 1997.

Heron, Onnaca. "The Lioness in the Text: Mary of Egypt as Immasculated Female Saint." *Quidditas* 21 (2000): 23–44.

Hill, Thomas D. "*Imago Dei:* Genre, Symbolism, and Anglo-Saxon Hagiography." In *Holy Men and Holy Women: Old English Prose Saints' Lives and Their Contexts*, edited by Paul E. Szarmach. SUNY Series in Medieval Studies. Albany, NY: State University of New York Press, 1996. 35–50.

Karras, Ruth Mazo. "Holy Harlots: Prostitute Saints in Medieval England." *Journal of the History of Sexuality* 1 (1990): 3–32.

Lavery, Simon. "The Story of Mary the Egyptian in Medieval England." In *The Legend of Mary of Egypt in Medieval Insular Hagiography*, edited by Erich Poppe and Bianca Ross. Dublin: Four Courts Press, 1996. 113–48.

Magennis, Hugh. "Conversion in Old English Saints' Lives." In *Essays on Anglo-Saxon and Related Themes in Memory of Lynne Grundy*, edited by Jane Roberts and Janet Nelson. King's College London Medieval Series 17. London: King's College London Centre for Late Antique and Medieval Studies, 2000. 287–310.

Magennis, Hugh. "St. Mary of Egypt and Aelfric: Unlikely Bedfellows in Cotton Julius E.vii?" In *The Legend of Mary of Egypt in Medieval Insular Hagiography*, edited by Erich Poppe and Bianca Ross. Dublin: Four Courts Press, 1996. 99–112.

"Mary of Egypt." In *The Oxford Dictionary of the Christian Church,* edited by F. L. Cross and E. A. Livingstone. Oxford: Oxford University Press, 1997.

Panagiotou, John G. "The Spiritual Desert of Our Times." *PEMPTOUSIA*. https://pemptousia.com. Accessed April 2, 2020.

Poppe, Erich, and Bianca Ross, eds. *The Legend of Mary of Egypt in Medieval Insular Hagiography.* Dublin: Four Courts Press, 1996.

Posa, Carmel M. "Mary and Zossima: Icons of Mutuality in the Spiritual Journey." *Tjurunga* 57 (1999): 5–21.

Roberts, Jane, and Janet Nelson, eds. *Essays on Anglo-Saxon and Related Themes in Memory of Lynne Grundy.* King's College London Medieval Series 17. London: King's College London Centre for Late Antiquity and Medieval Studies, 2000.

Scheil, Andrew P. "Bodies and Boundaries in the Old English Life of St. Mary of Egypt." *Neophilologus* 84 (2000): 137–56.

Skeat, Walter W., ed. *Aelfric's Lives of Saints.* Early English Text Society, OS 76, 82, 94, 114. London: Oxford University Press, 1881–1900.

Stevenson, Jane. "The Holy Sinner: The Life of Mary of Egypt." In *The Legend of Mary of Egypt in Medieval Insular Hagiography*, edited by Erich Poppe and Bianca Ross. Dublin: Four Courts Press, 1996. 19–50.

Szarmach, Paul E., ed. *Holy Men and Holy Women: Old English Prose Saints' Lives and Their Contexts.* SUNY Series in Medieval Studies. Albany: State University of New York Press, 1996.

Tristram, Hildegard L. C. Introduction to *The Legend of Mary of Egypt in Medieval Insular Hagiography*, edited by Erich Poppe and Bianca Ross. Dublin: Four Courts Press, 1996. 1–17.

Walsh, Efthalia Makris. "The Ascetic Mother Mary of Egypt." *The Greek Orthodox Theological Review* 34 (1989): 56–96.

Ward, Benedicta. "The Image of the Prostitute in the Middle Ages." *Monastic Studies* 16 (1985): 39–49.

Weiss, Judith. "The Metaphor of Madness in the Anglo-Norman Lives of St. Mary the Egyptian." In *The Legend of Mary of Egypt in Medieval Insular Hagiography*, edited by Erich Poppe and Bianca Ross. Dublin: Four Courts Press, 1996. 161–73.

Related Works

Although Saint Mary of Egypt probably postdates the desert Christians of the fourth century, knowledge of them immensely enhances understanding of her. Particularly helpful are the following works by Carrigan, Chitty, Merton, and Ward.

Alexandre, Monique. "Early Christian Women." In *A History of Women in the West: I. From Ancient Goddesses to Christian Saints,* edited by Pauline Schmitt Pantel. Cambridge, MA: The Belknap Press of Harvard University Press, 1992. 409–44, chap. 9.

Binns, John. *Ascetics and Ambassadors of Christ: The Monasteries of Palestine, 314–631.* Oxford: Clarendon, 1994.

Burrus, Virginia. *The Sex Lives of the Saints: An Erotics of Ancient Hagiography.* Philadelphia: University of Pennsylvania Press, 2004.

Burton-Christie, Douglas. *The Word in the Desert: Scripture and the Quest of Holiness in Early Christian Monasticism.* Oxford: Oxford University Press, 1993.

Carrigan, Henry L., Jr., ed. *Eternal Wisdom from the Desert.* Brewster, MA: Paraclete Press, 2001. Includes lives of Antony of Egypt and Paul of Thebes, and the Sayings of the Fathers.

Chitty, Derwas. *The Desert a City.* Oxford: Oxford University Press, 1966.

Dolger, Franz. "Byzantine Literature" (chapter XXVII). In *The Cambridge Medieval History,* Vol. IV, Part II, edited by J. M. Hussey. Cambridge: Cambridge University Press, 1967.

Egeria. *Diary of a Pilgrimage.* Trans. George E. Gingras. Ancient Christian Writers 38. New York: Newman Press, 1970.

Forman, Mary. *Praying with the Desert Mothers.* Collegeville, MN: Liturgical Press, 2005.

Hussey, J. M., ed. *The Cambridge Medieval History,* Vol. IV, Part II. Cambridge: Cambridge University Press, 1967.

Kadloubovsky, E., and G. E. H. Palmer, trans. *Writings from the Philokalia on Prayer of the Heart.* London: Faber & Faber, 1951/1983

Keller, David G. R. *Oasis of Wisdom (The Worlds of the Desert Fathe and Mothers).* Collegeville, MN: Liturgical Press, 2005.

Knowles, David. *Christian Monasticism.* New York: McGraw-Hill, 19 1977.

Lacarrière, Jacques. *The God-Possessed.* Trans. B. Arthaud. Lo George Allen & Unwin, 1963. Chaps. 4, 5, 7.

Louth, Andrew. *The Wilderness of God.* Nashville: Abingdon 1991. Chaps. 2, 3.

Merton, Thomas. *The Monastic Journey.* Ed. Br. Patrick Har City: Sheed, Andrews and McMeel, 1977.

Merton, Thomas. *Mystics and Zen Masters*. New York: Farrar, Straus and Giroux, 1961, 1987.

Merton, Thomas. *New Seeds of Contemplation*. New York: New Directions, 1961.

Merton, Thomas. *The Wisdom of the Desert*. New York: New Directions, 1960.

Norris, Kathleen. *The Cloister Walk*. New York: Riverhead Books, 1996.

Swan, Laura. *The Forgotten Desert Mothers*. New York: Paulist Press, 2001.

Waddell, Helen. *Beasts and Saints*. London: Constable and Company, 1934, 1953.

Ward, Benedicta. *The Desert Christian: The Sayings of the Desert Fathers*. New York: Macmillan, 1975.

Zernov, Nicolas. *Eastern Christendom*. London: Weidenfeld and Nicolson, 1961.